GW01338950

BERLIN AIRLIFT

The Effort and the Aircraft

OTHER WORKS BY JOHN PROVAN

Frankfurt International Airport: Portrait of an Airport in Europe
(Anton Plenk Verlag)

The German Airship in World War I
(Master's Thesis for University of Darmstadt)

The *Hindenburg* (CD-ROM) (Francis Verlag)

The Dornier Do-X (CD-ROM) (Francis Verlag)

OTHER BOOKS BY PALADWR PRESS

Davies and Machat full-color, fully-illustrated, series
Pan Am: An Airline and Its Aircraft
Lufthansa: An Airline and Its Aircraft
Delta: An Airline and Its Aircraft
Aeroflot: An Airline and Its Aircraft
Saudia: An Airline and Its Aircraft
TransBrasil: An Airline and Its Aircraft
Charles Lindbergh: An Airman, his Aircraft, and his Great Flights

Library Series
Fallacies and Fantasies of Air Transport History
For Pilot's Eyes Only
By Dead Reckoning
Fasten Your Seat Belts!
Pan Am's First Lady

Standard Davies Airline History Series
Airlines of the United States Since 1914
Airlines of Latin America Since 1919
Airlines of Asia Since 1920

Bibliography (2,700 titles)
Commercial Air Transport Books

BERLIN AIRLIFT
The Effort and the Aircraft

by John Provan
and *R.E.G. Davies*

Illustrated by *Mike Machat*

Paladwr Press

© 1998 John Provan and R.E.G. Davies

All rights reserved. No part of this publication, including photographs, maps, and artwork, may be reproduced or transmitted in any form or by any means, electronic or mechanical, including photocopy, recording, or any information storage and retrieval system, without the written permission of Paladwr Press.

Published by Paladwr Press, 1906 Wilson Lane, #101, McLean, Virginia 22102-1957, USA

Manufactured in Hong Kong

Book Design by R.E.G. Davies

Artwork by Mike Machat

Maps by R.E.G. Davies

Typesetting/Layout by Spot Color, Oakton, Virginia

Prepress and press management by The Drawing Board

ISBN 1-888962-05-4

First Edition

Contents

Foreword
by Dr. F. Robert van der Linden

Introduction..6–7

PRELUDE

The War Ends
New Frontiers
Black Market
Confrontation
The Airlift Begins . . .

The Soviet Empire......................8–9
Control Zones............................10–11
Currency Reform........................12–13
Berlin Isolated............................14–15
. . . With Vittles and Plainfare........16–17

AIRLIFT AIRCRAFT (U.S.)

The First Airlifters: Dakota . . .
General William Tunner
The Corridors
Skymaster . . .
Douglas C-74 Globemaster I
Boeing C-97 Stratofreighter
Getting Under Way
Combined Airlift Route Pattern

. . . and Skytrain.............................18–19
BEALCOM......................................20–21
Douglas C-54G Skymaster..............22–23
. . . Master of the Berlin Skies........24–25
Fairchild C-82 Packet.....................26–27
Douglas R5D (Naval C-54)..............28–29
British Commonwealth Support......30–31
The Berlin Approaches...................32–33

AIRLIFT AIRFIELDS

Berlin—Tempelhof
The Southern Corridor Fields
The Northern Corridor Fields
Maintenance
Airfield Construction
U.S. Scheduled Airline Help
Tunner's "Jungle Drums"

Berlin—Gatow and Tegel................34–35
The Central Corridor Fields............36–37
The Other Bases............................38–39
"90% of Aviation is on the Ground"..40–41
P.S.P., or the Marston Mat..............42–43
U.S. Non-Scheduled Airline Help....44–45
Marching to Different Drums.........46–47

AIRLIFT AIRCRAFT (BRITISH)

Bombers to Freighters
Avro Workhorses—Tudor . . .
The Air Tankers—Lancasters,
  Lincolns . . .
Passing the Salt—Sunderland
Answering the Call
The British Contribution

Handley Page Halifax/Halton.........48–49
. . . and York..................................50–51
. . . and Liberators.........................52–53
The Ubiquitous DC-3.....................54–55
The Spirit of Free Enterprise..........56–57
U.S. Spirit of Competition.............58–59

THE HUMAN SIDE OF THE AIRLIFT

The Human Touch
Operation Little Vittles
The Lighter Side
The Darker Side
Armed Forces Cooperation
The Siege and the Berliners
Things Could Have Been Worse

The Soldier's Life..........................60–61
The Candy Bomber.......................62–63
Airlift Laffs....................................64–65
British Problems...........................66–67
Vittles Statistics............................68–69
Sticking it Out...............................70–71
Other Sides of the Coin.................72–73

VICTORY

The Airlift Ends
Memorials
The Final Count

Reflections....................................74–75
The Spirit of Freedom...................76–77
Into the Book of Records..............78–79

Index..80

The endpapers of this book comprise (left) British artist Ronald Wong's splendid montage which encapsulates the many facets—military and human—of the Berlin Airlift; and (right) aviation master artist R.G. Smith's painting, which synthesizes the concentration of unprecedented air logistics activity—not to mention the uncertain weather. (Courtesy of Douglas/Boeing)

Foreword by Dr. F. Robert van der Linden

Fifty years ago the world was pushed to the brink of war. On June 24, 1948, the Soviet Union sealed off the divided city of Berlin, escalating the already extreme tensions of the brewing Cold War. Only three years since the United States and the Soviet Union had fought together to destroy Nazi Germany, the former Allies now found themselves to be opponents in Greece, China, and eastern Europe.

For President Harry S Truman, his doctrine of containment and brinkmanship sought to block Soviet expansion; for General Secretary Joseph Stalin, however, the Western Allies were attempting to strangle the Soviet Union, to destroy the Revolution and worse, to rebuild Germany, its traditional enemy. These conflicting perceptions now came to a head in occupied Germany in response to the mounting currency crisis. Citing "technical problems," the Soviet army blocked road and rail access into the western zone of Berlin, some 80 miles inside Soviet-held territory. Complying to the letter of an earlier agreement, they did not block access by air, thinking that the Western Allies had neither the stomach nor the capability to supply a city of 2.4 million strictly by airlift.

While many in the West did waver, General Lucius D. Clay and President Truman did not. For almost 18 months, all the needs of the former German capital were met through the largest airlift in history. The United States and Great Britain, with the technical support of France, did the impossible. They supplied the basic needs of an entire metropolis from the air. By May of 1949, the Soviets admitted failure and reopened road and rail service to Berlin. The Western Allies continued the Airlift until September, just in case the Soviets encountered further "technical problems" in the coming winter months. The victory of the Berlin Airlift for the West set the tone of the Cold War for decades to come. The outcome divided Europe for half a century and did much to change the West's perception of western Germany from a defeated enemy to a friendly ally.

In 1984, as a curator in the Aeronautics Department of the National Air and Space Museum, I was assigned a project to prepare an exhibit commemorating the 100th anniversary of the birth of President Harry Truman. Clearly the aviation highlight of his career was the triumph of the Berlin Airlift. He it was who ultimately rebuffed Soviet coercion, stating bluntly in his direct Missourian manner, "We stay in Berlin, period." And stay he did.

In my research for the exhibit I discovered volumes on the diplomatic and political background to the conflict. The biographies have been written, the analyses have been made, but what I found lacking was a single reference that addressed the most important aspect of the Airlift—aviation. Aside from the excellent but difficult-to-find official histories of the Airlift prepared by the air forces of the United States and Great Britain, there is little material except in eclectic periodicals to cover this most critical story. This concise volume by John Provan and Ron Davies capably remedies this oversight.

This work, well illustrated with photographs from John Provan's personal collection together with the stunning aircraft drawings of Mike Machat and the richly informative maps of Ron Davies, provides an excellent primer for the interested reader who seeks a well-balanced single-volume reference on the Berlin Airlift. This succinct book provides a thorough overview of the history of the Airlift, replete with numerous interesting vignettes that provide a human face to the story. The product of comprehensive research and careful editing, it highlights the triumphs and tragedies of this landmark event, underscoring the story of one of the greatest demonstrations of military air power in history—a victory without guns.

Frau Louise Schroeder preceded Ernst Reuter as Mayor of Berlin, and, in the winter of 1947/48 laid the foundations of a rationing system on an equitable basis.

Ernst Reuter succeeded Schroeder, arriving back in Berlin in 1948 after self-enforced exile in Turkey, where he had found refuge from the Nazis.

Author's Preface

For years I have researched the history of the Flug and Luftschiffhafen (Air and Airship Station) Rhein-Main and its role in the development of German rigid airships. Eight years ago, during an open house at Rhein-Main Air Base, I had the opportunity to meet Gail Halvorsen, the "Candy Bomber." He was very interested in my explanation of the airship history of the base, and the meeting served to awaken my curiosity about the role that Rhein-Main played during the Berlin Airlift.

The stories he told were moving, stimulating, and emotional, so much so that they encouraged me to research the topic. These researches included many interviews and contacts with people who took part in that remarkable exercise in aviation logistics, no less than half a century ago. These people are quite old today, but their spirit is still young, and that spirit was outstandingly in evidence during the Berlin Airlift of 1948–49.

Although I was aware of many other books and writings on the subject, I felt that this historic example of humanitarian aid had not been presented in its full perspective. And so, with Ron Davies's help, I wrote this book, which describes the many different aspects and features of the Airlift, not only of the airmen, the aircraft, and the airfields—although these are well covered—but also the causes and the consequences.

The Berlin Airlift served as a test-bed or training ground for many innovations in aviation practice that came into general use afterwards. The Airlift helped to accelerate the development of cargo-handling practices and routines, emphasized the efficiency of large aircraft and the need for paved runways, and revealed the full potential of radar as a superb navigational aid. In this sense, the Airlift can be said to have given strength to the axiom that Necessity is the Mother of Invention.

John Provan

Introduction

Artist's Note
This book has been a slight modification of my normal assignment to illustrate Ron Davies's airline books. The list of required aircraft drawings this time was, as usual, of transport types; but most of them were military versions of those types. Thus the choice of, for instance, U.S.A.F. and R.A.F. aircraft, together with the American and British civilian companies, demanded a different line of research. To locate authentic color schemes of a small British charter operator that perhaps lasted only a few months, and whose aircraft may or may not have been painted, 50 years ago, in any color scheme at all, was not easy.

The U.S.A.F.'s hastily-assembled fleet of more than 300 Douglas C-54s included aircraft with many different paint schemes. We made a selection that seemed to be representative and have illustrated five different ones, as well as that of a U.S. Navy R5D variant of the basic Douglas DC-4 design. Similarly, the venerable Douglas C-47, military version of the famous DC-3, is shown in the markings of both the U.S.A.F. and the R.A.F., as a matching pair; and one in unusual markings.

The drawings of the civilian carriers—non-scheduled operators such as Alaska or Seaboard & Western from the U.S., and Skyways, Silver City, or Flight Refuelling from Great Britain, help to emphasize that the Berlin Airlift really was an Allied team effort. All concerned parties contributed in any way possible to meet the emergency.

In the case of the British types, these were, as often as not, post-war conversions of the famous Lancaster and Halifax bombers; while the salt-carrying Sunderland was a reminder that the Berlin Airlift was also served by a few flying boats as well as landplanes. And although, from my point of view as an artist, they often appear clumsy, the old bombers did the job. Quite surprisingly, the ill-fated Tudor, regarded as an ugly duckling by many, was a great load-carrier, especially of oil and gasoline. And once off the ground, it does not look too bad either.

Indeed, for the dust jacket, a British independent operator (i.e., not one of the state corporations) was chosen, so that Eagle Aviation's Red Eagle could add to the cover a welcome flash of color, reflecting what it must have done when in action: to brighten up what was usually a drab airfield scene, populated by drab all-metal aircraft.

Customarily in these books, I make a comment on "Machat's Law," to the effect that no two individual aircraft of a single type in an airline fleet are ever painted exactly the same. In the case of the Berlin Airlift, this comment would seem to be superfluous, if only because of the nose-art.

Mike Machat

Publisher's Note
When John Provan approached me to enquire about publishing his book on The Berlin Airlift, I was intrigued. I knew John as an indefatigable and meticulous researcher, who had already produced encyclopaedic tomes on the Zeppelins and their sheds. His approach led to a meeting, at which he presented the results of his Berlin researches, together with an album of photographs, many of which had been obtained from former Airlift participants.

He did not claim that his story would contain much that had not been written about before; but it had never been presented in the Paladwr Press style, with Mike Machat's immaculate aircraft profile drawings, nor with sufficient cartographic work to supplement the text. Many Airlift photographs have been reproduced in magazines and reports; but many of John's had not, especially the colored ones.

John was tolerant of my editing, as I modified his narrative into the Paladwr Press style—and added a little of my own, especially at the beginning—for most Airlift books and monographs do not deal adequately with the events that led, first to the Blockade, then to the Airlift itself.

As with previous Paladwr books, we have interwoven text, drawings, maps, photographs, and tabulations into a cohesive whole; and at the same time arranged the material in such a way that the two-page spreads can be perused individually as self-contained episodes or commentaries, in what may be termed "book-bites." These can be selected at random; yet, at the same time, the chronology of the Airlift is preserved. Thus the reader can pick up the book for a short-term read; or take it as a whole.

Paladwr Press has tried to emphasize that the Berlin Airlift was a combined Allied effort. Unfortunately, some publications have presented the Airlift story simply as an American accomplishment; others have done the opposite. The U.S. carried most of the coal, and the flour, and the potatoes, accounting for the majority of the tonnage; but the British carried the liquid fuel, the salt, the fish, and most of the returning passengers. While there was competition, this was of friendly rivalry, all directed at a common cause, a supreme humanitarian enterprise.

Rather like the Lindbergh book, this is a departure from our routine subject material, customarily of a single airline. But Paladwr thought that the Berlin Airlift deserved special treatment, including a double-gate-fold map to show that the Airlift began as far west as California. And there are some little-known Machat specials to delight the eye.

R.E.G. Davies

Acknowledgements
Many individuals assisted in making this book possible. Gail Halvorsen was my inspiration for tackling the subject, with his stories of countless Berliners who remembered his candy drops. James Spatafora (known as Spat) a Rhein-Main Berlin Airlift veteran, supplied many stories and photographs. Countless other veterans or their wives provided photographs and information. Thanks especially to Robert Ausdell, John Banasick, Harvey Clark, Albert Lowe, Robert Pine, Don Schoonover, Jim "Jake" Schuffert, and Gloria Wenk for sharing her slides, bringing much color into the story. Liv Atgeltinger, Norway, was very helpful and, Jack Bennett in Berlin was always at hand, as were Gerd and Gerdi Rausch, and Dr. Michael Wustrack, Frankfurt International Airport. Mr. Krause, Flughafen Hamburg, also provided photographs. Mrs. Lois Walker and Dr. Dan Harrington, U.S. Air Force Historians, Ramstein A.B., provided a wealth of information, greatly assisted in proofreading, and provided many suggestions. The Commanders, men, and women of Rhein-Main A.B. were always very helpful, with special thanks to Dave Jablonski, at the Public Affairs Office. The staff of the National Archives, Washington D.C., uncovered many forgotten photos. Helga Mellmann, from Berlin, saved countless photos from destruction when Tempelhof A.B. closed down. Mrs. Helga Pförter, Archivist for the BEWAG Co. in Berlin was very helpful. Georg Wolf, Glasofen and Andreas Schleifer, Frankfurt, assisted with photographic reproductions. Alex Herz provided much helpful information about R.A.F. Schleswigland. Captain Grötte, Lufttransportgeschwader 62, Harry Holmes, and Mr. Vorholt assisted with photos from R.A.F. Wunstorf, and Alfred Fries with material from Hamburg. Thanks also to Barry Countryman. Nick Forder supplied information about Operation Plainfare and R.A.F. aircraft. A number of organizations were very supportive in this book: Lutz Caspers from the American Friends Service Committee (the Quakers), Neustedt; Howard Hatch from the Church of Jesus Christ of Latter Day Saints; Mrs. Inge Lather from CARE Deutschland; and Pedro Soto from CARE USA.

My wife, Helga, deserves special thanks for her kind understanding and assisting in my research and proofreading. Special thanks to Ron Davies, Sam Smith, Simine Short, John Wegg, and Bob van der Linden, and Guy Halford-McLeod who carefully corrected, and shaped this manuscript for publication. Without such support and much more, this project could not have been realized. Thank you all.

John Provan

The War Ends

Demobilization
The Second World War left much of Europe in ruin and ashes. Six long years of fighting had cost the lives of millions. Polarized emotions, distrust, and insecurity were widespread among all the peoples of Europe.

After the end of the war, the United States, Great Britain, and the British Commonwealth began the massive task of demobilization into civilian life of some 8 million soldiers, sailors and airmen. Hundreds of thousands of jeeps, trucks, and tanks were scrapped or sold. The same fate awaited the huge fleet of aircraft that once covered the skies. Most of the bombers were scrapped and many cargo aircraft sold, often very inexpensively, to hastily-organized charter airlines or to private owners. Such availability of aircraft and trained pilots helped in the rapid expansion of civil aviation in the United States, while the U.S. Army Air Forces shrank to a small fraction of their former size. In Great Britain, old bombers were converted for passenger or cargo use. They were operated by the three state corporations and also by the independent non-scheduled airlines.

Demoralization
On the civilian front, the ravages of war took a heavy toll. A Europe that had, by the late 1930s, enjoyed high standards of living, thanks to efficient agriculture and vigorous manufacturing and commerce, was now in desperate straits. Even in formerly prosperous industrial areas, ordinary people lived, almost hand-to-mouth, at least in the months immediately after the war ended in the late spring of 1945. Every day was spent in search of food and the other necessities of life, and in the big cities especially, the bomb damage was such that clearing the rubble was a major undertaking, even before any thought of rebuilding could begin. Interestingly, much of the rubble was put to good use—as the hard-core base for new runways at the airfields.

Nazi aggression, especially the bombing of Britain, led to devastating retaliation. The whole city was a mass of ruins in 1945, and this picture, taken in 1947, looking towards the Brandenburg Gate, emphasizes that the damage to the city was measured not only in rubble but in the absence of normal traffic on the often deserted streets. (Schoonover)

Transport in Frankfurt was almost at a standstill, except for the resilient streetcars and Allied army vehicles.

There was little to buy in the shops, and often there were no shops. (These pictures courtesy U.S. Army Signal Corps)

The civilian population lived, at least for two or three years, under strict control of almost all walks of life.

The Soviet Empire

A Triumphant Power
When the Red Army soldier planted the hammer-and-sickle flag on the top of the Reichstag, the nominal seat of government of a defeated Germany, the symbolism was more far-reaching than that of a military victory. From a nation that, in 1940, still lagged behind capitalist countries in demonstrable achievement, it had, by enormous effort and sacrifice, poured all its strength into the war, with such effect that it overcame the might of the German armed forces on land and in the air, to emerge in 1945 as a world power, militarily on a par with the United States, and capable of spreading the influence of communism throughout the world.

Bitter Memories
Indeed, there were indications of such a spread of political dogma, as the countries surrounding the Soviet Union were obliged to toe the communist line, with Soviet occupation troops to ensure that they did so. While such dominance was mainly expansionistic, it was partly in self-defence. Throughout history, Russia had experienced threats or invasions from the west. The Teutonic Knights in the 13th, Poland and Lithuania in the 14th, and Sweden in the 18th centuries, had all invaded Russia from the west. Napoleon reached the gates of Moscow in 1812; Imperialist Germany might well have done so, but for the Treaty of Brest Litovsk in 1918; and in 1941, Hitler's panzer divisions were almost within sight of the Kremlin's spires. In the last case, the murder, rape, pillage, and destruction that accompanied the Blitzkrieg invasion—an estimated 20 million Russians were killed—left an almost irreparable and indelible mark in Russian minds.

Cordon Sanitaire
While many post-war months were to pass before the 'Iron Curtain' was drawn across the center of Europe, to divide it into the capitalist west and the communist east, the Soviet Union was apprehensive of the intentions of the western powers, even though such fears were unfounded. The sense of self-preservation took the form of ensuring that all the countries on its frontiers were allied, friendly, or at the very least, non-aggressive and unlikely to pose a threat.

By 1949, the ring of buffer states would be almost complete, to establish a *cordon sanitaire* of protective territory along all the potentially vulnerable frontier zones of the Union of Soviet Socialist Republics (U.S.S.R.).

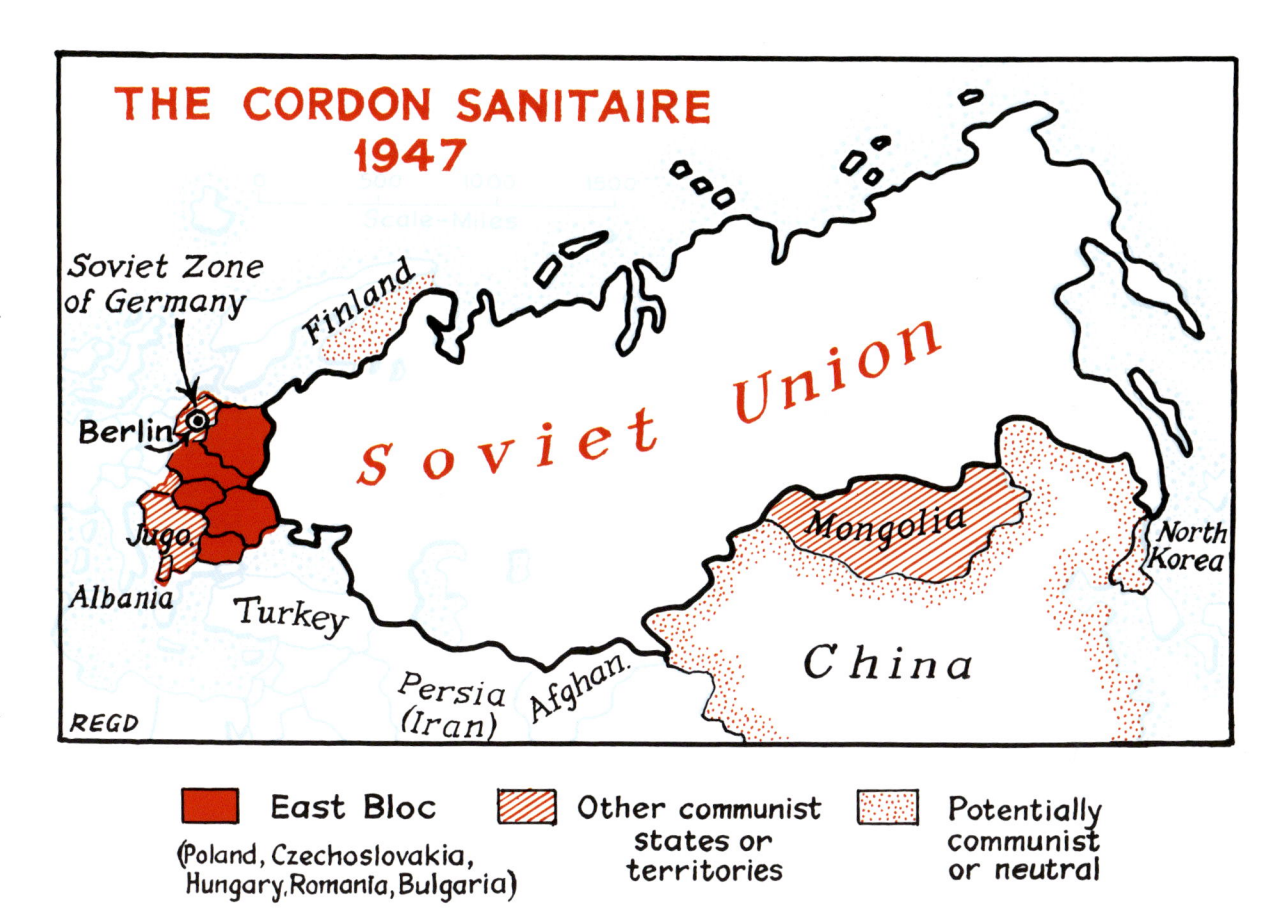

In Eastern Europe, all the neighboring countries were to have communist governments, and could have been forced into their adoption by the military, if necessary. Finland was not a military threat, and the three Baltic states had been annexed. In the Asiatic Far East, Mongolia and North Korea were effectively puppet states, though nominally independent, and China was about to become communist. In the south, Iran and Afghanistan were neutral, and Turkey was leaning towards the West. The Soviet Union was constantly alert to any potential threat to its borders.

Too Close for Comfort?
With its Zone of Occupation of Germany including Berlin, Josef Stalin was no doubt particularly sensitive to any signs of intrusion from the capitalist west. More than half of Berlin consisted of the American, British, and French Zones of Occupation (see page 11). The northern fringe of Berlin was a bare 30 miles from the Polish frontier, so that the capitalist enclave, in the eyes of the Russians, seemed to be an uncomfortable irritant.

New Frontiers

Expansion of the Third Reich
In less than two years, after the annexation of Austria in March 1938, Hitler's Germany almost doubled in size. The Sudetenland of Czechoslovakia was taken over in September 1938, and the country itself was dissolved in March 1939, with Bohemia and Moravia declared 'protectorates,' and Slovakia given nominal independence. Germany and the U.S.S.R. invaded Poland in September 1939, starting the Second World War. Simultaneously, the notorious Molotov-Ribbentrop pact between the U.S.S.R. and Germany seemed at the time to be a political masterstroke, as Germany's eastern front was neutralized, a situation that prevailed until Germany invaded the U.S.S.R. in June 1941. The direct result was that (not for the first time in history) Poland was partitioned and disappeared as an independent nation.

Collapse of Germany
When the War ended in May 1945, the victorious nations more than cancelled out the territorial gains of 1938–39. Austria and Czechoslovakia, though occupied, regained their independence, and Poland also regained its nationhood, albeit at substantial sacrifice. Its frontiers were completely changed. In compensation for about 70,000 square miles of territory ceded to the U.S.S.R., Poland received about 40,000 square miles of eastern Germany, east of the so-called Oder-Neisse Line (named after the rivers that formed the new frontier). This new territory included Pomerania, part of Prussia, and the industrial area of Silesia. The former League of Nations free zone of Danzig became the Polish Gdansk, and the 'Polish Corridor,' formerly Poland's only access to the Baltic Sea, expanded to a Baltic coastline almost as long as Germany's.

Control Zones

Back to Politics
The political situation within Europe in the late 1940s was tense. To win the war, the Western Allies had formed a military alliance with the U.S.S.R. Political and ideological differences had been set aside for the common goal of victory. With this objective now achieved, the ideological differences between democracy and communism surfaced, with each side attempting to gain popularity among the populations of the nations of Europe. Though defeated, Germany was especially important because of its industrial and strategic potential. In the following years, the city of Berlin was to play an ever more important symbolic role.

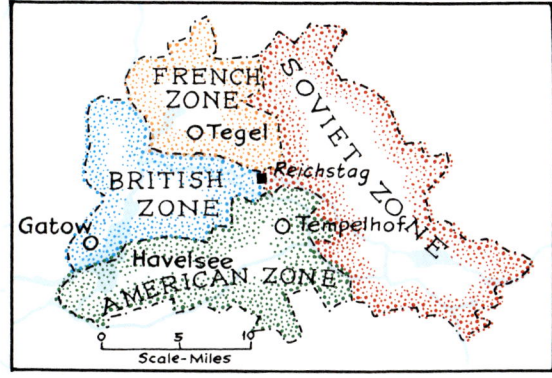

A Nation Divided
The Soviet Red Army had fought a bitter battle to take Berlin and it considered the city to be within its sphere of influence. The four powers had agreed to geographical boundaries, which divided Germany into four occupation, or control zones. Berlin was located within the Soviet zone, but the city would also be divided into four sectors. The Western Allies had halted their advance into Germany and even removed their troops from the Soviet zone under the terms agreed upon. Although hostilities ended on 8 May 1945, the U.S. and British forces had not been allowed by the Soviets to enter the city of Berlin itself until 2 July 1945, when elements of the U.S. 2nd Armored Division arrived, with headquarters on Kronprinzenallee in Berlin. The Russian military headquarters was located at Babelsberg, 10 miles east of Berlin and were known as the Little Kremlin. Headquarters of the Allied Control were located at Elszholzstrasse in a large 550-room former palace.

Cold City
Like most of Germany, Berlin had suffered catastrophic damage during the war. The devastating effects of round-the-clock bombing and the Soviet ground assault had left the city in ruins. 70% of all buildings were either destroyed or badly damaged. One-third of the population had either fled or been killed. The remainder comprised women, children, and the elderly, while the majority of the male population was interned in P.O.W. (Prisoners of War) camps, located far and wide. During the harsh winter of 1946/47, people froze to death because of the lack of heat and nourishment. One Berliner chalked on a wall of a government building; "Blessed are the dead, for their hands do not freeze."

A mass influx of refugees into Germany was caused by 10.7 million Germans from Poland and another 2.9 million from Czechoslovakia, leading to much privation, even hunger. The eastern portion of Germany, most of which was now in Poland, had been the bread basket of the country, supplying the majority of food, while the western portion was mainly industrial and was unable to feed adequately the influx of additional population.

Free Elections
Under the terms of the **Potsdam Agreement,** the formation of political parties within Germany was permitted. The United States was convinced that this would lead Germany to democracy, while the Soviets were confident that the Germans would follow a single party, the communists. On 10 June 1945, the Soviets formed the K.P.D. (German Communist Party), in the Soviet part of Germany, making a head start in the new political arena. The K.P.D. later became the S.E.D. (Sozialistische Einheits Partei—the Socialist Unity Party). Soviet control of the media in the eastern sector of Berlin was thought to ensure communist victory in the upcoming elections. But on 20 October 1946, the Berlin elections provided the first major disappointment for the Soviet leadership, when the S.P.D. (Social Democratic Party of Germany) won 48%, C.D.U. (Christian Democratic Union), 22%, and the S.E.D. only 19% of the votes. These elections demonstrated that total Soviet control could not be achieved by political means. **Ernst Reuter** (29 July 1889–29 September 1953) was elected Lord Mayor by the City Assembly of Berlin, only to be vetoed by the Soviets. The split between East and West was widening, and before new elections (scheduled for December 1948) could be held, the blockade would begin and Reuter would be elected unilaterally to become an important figure among the population of Berlin. **General Lucius D. Clay,** (23 April 1897–16 April 1978) had been named the U.S. Military Governor of Occupied Germany on 15 March 1947. The State Department was to develop American policy and the U.S. Army was to execute it but this arrangement did not always work in practice. Reuter's support and friendship during the Airlift would play a critical role.

The Soviets had dismantled a substantial portion of Germany's industry and resources in an attempt to assist their own war-torn nation and partly by a harsh program of reparations. Before the American forces were allowed to enter Berlin, the Russians had transported some 10,000 railroad cars of goods to the Soviet Union.

Black Market

Black Market
The old Reichs Mark remained the official currency of Germany, although the national state it represented, Hitler's Third Reich, no longer existed. The shortage of goods available in Germany during the war, along with full employment required for the war effort and high wages, resulted in excess purchasing power, held by the general population in liquid savings, thus creating an almost worthless currency. There was nothing to buy, yet everyone had plenty of money. The black market and the value of cigarettes replaced the worthless Reichs Mark as a means of exchange. A Bechstein grand piano would cost sixteen cartons of cigarettes and a small bar of Hershey's chocolate commanded 30 marks ($20 in today's equivalent currency).

Barter Market
In an attempt to stamp out the black market, the Office of Military Government, United States (OMGUS) set up a barter market system in 1946-47. American military personnel and civilians could bring food, clothing, etc. to local barter centers, where the objects would be appraised into credit slips. With these, Americans could buy objects such as crystal, cameras, etc., that had also been appraised. The Germans would then buy items, such as food or clothing which they needed, using their credit slips. This barter system aided everyone and was legal.

Street Market
The black market was commonplace. Trading went on quite openly, and it was impossible to distinguish between legitimate exchanges and the crooked. A mother could not be deterred from selling a clock or a camera so as to buy food. 9,000 German policemen were used to man the border sector of Berlin, in an attempt to control large-scale black market activities and were especially successful in March and April 1949, when during 32 raids, they seized goods such as cigarettes, coffee, shoes, CARE packages, gold, and money with a total value of more than 1 million West Marks. Several items were in short supply in the Soviet sector, such as medicines, so that some Berliners would cross over and trade these for food or fuel. These items would often be hidden in the arms of a coat or inside the legs of pants.

The prominent warning notices apparently had little effect as soldiers (on all sides of the sector lines) indulged in some mutually profitable bartering. (U.S. Army Corps of Engineers)

The 'black' market was so much a part of life of post-war Germany that it took the form of an almost legitimized street market. No doubt the traders were highly mobile and irrepressible enough to evade even the most assiduous police control.

Currency Reform

The Bi-Zone
On 30 July 1946, the American and British occupation zones were economically merged into the Bi-Zone, effective in January 1947, with the French joining in on 20 April 1948.

Incidentally, **the U.S. Air Force** was created on 18 September 1947 as a separate military organization. President Harry S Truman had signed a proclamation commemorating the 40th anniversary of the Army Air Force on 1 August 1947. Eleven months later, the newly-formed U.S.A.F. would face its first major challenge.

The Marshall Plan
Early in 1947, President Truman established the **Marshall Plan,** to assist the nations of Europe in economic reconstruction. At a meeting in Paris, from 12 July to 22 September 1947, sixteen nations considered the program. The western European nations accepted the plan; but the Soviets, who had suffered badly at the hands of the Germans, with an estimated 20 million people killed, did not. The Soviets opposed the survival of capitalism among European nations and a loss in their power and prestige. In protest, the Soviet Military Governor, Marshal Vassily Danilovich Sokolowsky, walked out of the Allied Control Council in Berlin on 20 March 1948.

Operation Bird Dog
For the Marshall Plan to work, a totally new currency had to be introduced in Germany. A Council of Foreign Ministers met in London in December 1947 to consider the situation. The Soviet government disagreed. Nevertheless, the new money was secretly printed by the U.S. Treasury Department in Washington D.C., and transported in 23,000 boxes, weighing 1,035 tons, to the old Reichsbank building in Frankfurt/Main. The project was called **Operation Bird Dog** and General Clay was given the discretion as to the timing of the currency's release. The Russians had no idea about the new currency as late as 17 June 1948.

On Friday, 18 June, after all banks had closed for the weekend, the official announcement was made. The **Bank Deutscher Länder** was established as the central bank for the Western zones. On Sunday, 20 June, the new currency was introduced within the western zones of Germany, while talks were still under way about Berlin. By 23 June, General Clay refused the Soviet idea of allowing an 'East' German Mark to be the sole currency for Berlin. The new notes introduced in Berlin were stamped with a red B for Berlin, which was a precautionary measure to control the flow of currency (repeating a concept used during the war, when U.S. dollars issued for the Hawaiian Islands were overprinted 'Hawaii') The German currency reform was a comprehensive and complicated restructuring of wages, prices, public and private debt, exchange rates, and banking regulations. The reform was not simply a revaluation. Wages and salaries acquired a genuine purchasing power, because products suddenly became more available.

On Wednesday, 23 June 1948, the Soviet military announced currency reform for all Soviet zones. This was very makeshift, as the old Third Reich currency was reissued with a Soviet Zone Monetary Reform Coupon placed at the left corner. The Soviets did not have the time to print new bills to prevent huge amounts of former Reichs Marks from entering the Eastern zone, by people from the West attempting to buy goods with the now worthless Reichs Marks. A short time later, the Soviets introduced their new currency for the eastern zone of Germany.

(To complicate the situation, the United States had issued what was called **Allied Occupation Currency (Allierte Militärbehörde Geld).** Unfortunately, they also gave the Soviets a set of printing plates. To pay their troops, the Soviet government began to print huge uncontrolled amounts of this currency. Although it was intended for Allied use, distrust arose and the use of the old Reichs Mark and cigarettes continued.)

Reconstruction Plan
By June 1948, the United States, Great Britain, and France had agreed to a five-point plan for Germany's reconstruction. (1) Germany would become a republic and a German assembly would write a new democratic constitution; (2) The Allies would integrate this new republic into the western European economies; (3) The West German Republic would include the industrial region of the Ruhr valley; (4) The United States would station troops in Germany for an indefinite period of time; and (5) The Allied powers would cooperate closely and coordinate the economic policies in their sectors of Germany. The currency reform therefore played an important role for points 2 and 5.

To reissue an entirely new currency is no easy task. This scene is at the Reichsbank in Frankfurt, where enormous stacks of superseded notes had to be counted. (U.S. Army Signal Corps)

Confrontation

Limited Access to Berlin
Although the division of Berlin into four sectors had been agreed upon at Potsdam in 1945, the terms of access remained legally open as the Soviet government refused to sign any such agreements. **Marshal Georgi K. Zhukov,** Soviet commander in Germany, had verbally promised General Clay the use of a major highway and rail line into Berlin, but Clay never pressed for a written agreement, fearing limitations of American rights in the city. There were ominous signs that the Soviets were making difficulties at the road and rail frontier control points into their zone. An air safety agreement had been signed on 30 November 1945, which legitimized the use of three air corridors to Berlin.

Warning Shots
On Monday, 31 March 1948, in a gesture of provocation, three U.S. military trains were detained by the Soviets. General Clay ordered all such trains to be stopped and all personnel airlifted. Clay asked Colonel Henry Dorr (commander of Tempelhof A.B. (Air Base)) how many C-47 aircraft were available at Frankfurt's Rhein-Main A.B. Dorr answered "36 planes, but because of overhauls, only 25 are operational."

Clay's Pigeons
Sixty tons of the most essential supplies were trucked to Rhein-Main A.B. and before midnight 2 April, Operation Little Lift began. The **U.S. Air Forces in Europe (U.S.A.F.E.)** had been redesignated and activated on 16 August 1945. Formerly known as U.S. Strategic Air Forces in Europe, it flew about 300 tons of supplies for the military garrison in Berlin during Operation Little Lift, which lasted about ten days. Pilots and crews volunteered to fly the night missions to Berlin, apparently unconcerned that Russian Yak-3 fighters could easily destroy the unarmed C-47s. Lieut. Vernon Hamman recalled, "We were so young and so dumb, all of us volunteered." These pilots later received the nickname: 'Clay's Pigeons.'

Growing Irritations
An unusual "milk affair" occurred on 17 April 1948. After the war, the Russians had rounded up 7,000 dairy cows in the Berlin area and moved them into the Soviet sector. For years the Russians had supplied the Allies with 18,000 quarts daily, in exchange for a daily supply of American flour. Now the Soviets claimed that a lack of trucks prevented them from supplying the milk and the Americans should transport it. The Americans were forced to agree.

Between 17 April and 23 June, 2,000 students revolted against communist control of the Humboldt, the only university in Berlin, but which was in the Soviet sector. Reuter helped in creating the Free University of Berlin, which opened on 8 November 1948. These actions increased tensions but the situation came to a head because of the economic policies undertaken by the West.

Furthermore, this was against the background of what became known as the Cold War, and Europe as a whole was fast becoming two sharply defined areas, politically and culturally, divided by a recognizable frontier zone which Winston Churchill named the Iron Curtain.

General Lucius DuBignon Clay, U.S. Military Governor of Germany. (U.S. Army Signal Corps)

The Douglas C-47 (military version of the commercial DC-3), which had been the workhorse transport aircraft throughout the Second World War, was quickly drafted into service again with the emergency created by the Berlin blockade. (U.S.A.F.)

Berlin Isolated

The Blockade Begins
At midnight on 23 June 1948, in an effort to dilute the western Allies' influence in Berlin; the Soviets began to cut electric power and at 6 a.m. the next day, they halted all civilian road, rail, and barge traffic. Some military traffic, for essential needs only, was still able to continue by the autobahnen; and one military train left Berlin at 8 p.m. every evening. Marshal Sokolowsky later announced that the Kommandatura (the joint military headquarters for the four powers in Berlin) no longer existed. The Berlin blockade had begun.

Gen. Clay had convinced President Truman of the necessity of defending and remaining in Berlin. A U.S. withdrawal from Berlin would have been a massive loss in prestige for the Western powers. Germany was symbolic of the Cold War and Berlin was a microcosm of Germany.

Air Strength Imbalance
The western Allies were unprepared. Since the end of World War Two, the armed forces had been greatly reduced. The Soviets, on the other hand, maintained their huge military force and were in a far better position for conflict. U.S.A.F.E. had only eleven operational groups, with 275 aircraft, mostly light bombers or fighters and the situation in Great Britain was no better. The Soviet Air Force had some 4,000 aircraft, two-thirds of which were in Germany. The Soviets were unlikely to have wished to start a war, and ample opportunities to provoke a conflict had occurred. Nevertheless, no chances were taken on either side.

Deterrent
To create a military balance, President Truman ordered sixty long-range B-29 Superfortress aircraft, theoretically equipped with atomic bombs, to Marham (Norfolk), Lakenheath (Suffolk), and Waddington (Lincolnshire) bases in England. Unknown to the Soviets, atomic bombs were scarce and these B-29s had not even been modified to carry them. The Western military presence in Berlin was far from adequate. 3,000 American, 2,000 British and 1,500 French troops were positioned there. On the other side, the Soviets had 18,000 troops in Berlin and thousands more within their zone. For the first time since 1945, the American military was ready to use the atomic bomb as a deterrent, at least in theory. The Soviets, however, would not successfully develop and detonate an atomic bomb until August 1949. The atomic threat was enough to prevent them from considering a massive military action against Berlin.

Preparation
The maintenance base at Burtonwood in Lancashire was reopened to repair the B-29s. Even with conventional bombs, these B-29 aircraft could have attacked locations deep within the Soviet Union. The entire action was called Project Skincoat.

Along with the B-29s, 16 Lockheed F-80 Shooting Stars, the first operational U.S. jet fighter aircraft, from the 56th Fighter Group, were transferred from Selfridge Field, Michigan, to Germany. On 14 August 1948, 75 more F-80s arrived in Europe on the aircraft carrier *USS Sicily*. The general public was not usually made aware of these military preparations for conflict.

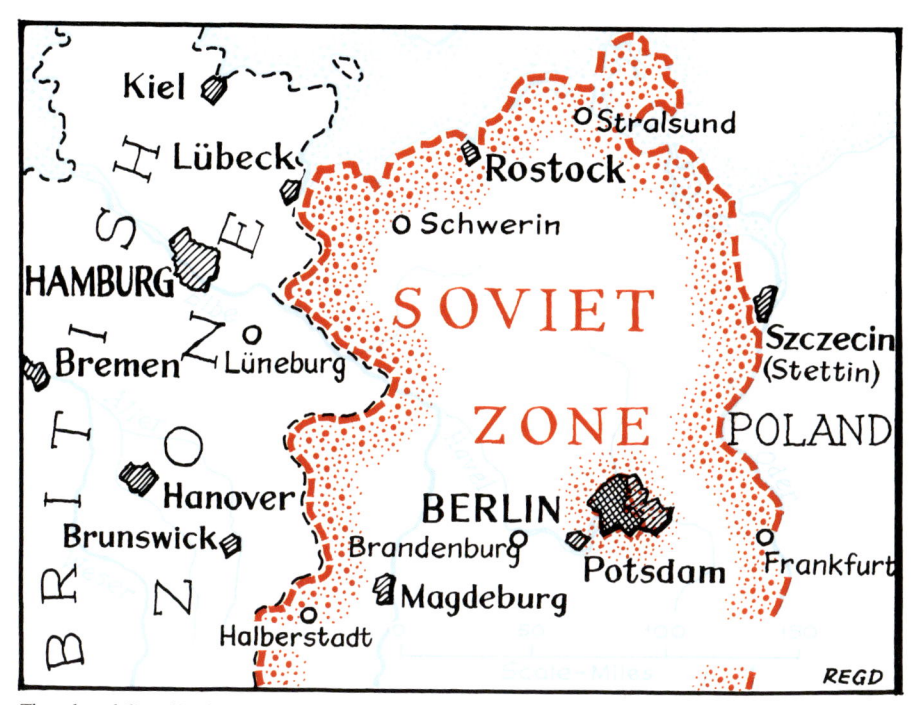

The vulnerability of Berlin is not always fully appreciated. Surrounded on all sides by the Soviet Zone and Red Army-controlled Poland, it was 150 miles from its traditional port of Hamburg, 80 miles from the British Zone frontier, and a mere 30 miles from Poland.

A road from the British zone completely blocked—and not only by the level-crossing (grade crossing) style gates. (U.S. Army Signal Corps)

The Airlift Begins . . .

The idea of supplying the Berliners, as well as the British occupation troops, by air, was first suggested by **Air Commodore C.N. Waite**, of the Royal Air Force, who put forward a plan to General Sir Brian Robertson, who passed this on to General Clay.

Before the blockade, Berlin imported 15,500 tons of supplies every day to meet its needs, a minimum of 4,000 tons daily were required to survive. In the beginning the U.S.A.F. could only supply 700 tons. A rationing system in Berlin was instituted within two days of the blockade, which included 75% of nonessential industries being deprived of electric power.

"Let Battle Commence"
General Clay called **Lieutenant General Curtis E. LeMay,** Commander-in-Chief, U.S.A.F.E.. "Curt," said General Clay, "can you transport coal by air?" LeMay answered: "How much coal do you want to haul?" Clay answered "All you can." Thus, the Berlin Airlift, at first called "LeMay's Coal and Feed Company—Round-the-Clock Service Guaranteed," started when the 61st Troop Carrier Group stationed at Rhein-Main Air Base began with only 25 C-47 aircraft to airlift supplies to Berlin.

Brigadier General Joseph Smith was initially placed in command of the Airlift and gave the Berlin Airlift its name, albeit an unofficial one, **Operation Vittles,** "since we're hauling grub," as he once said. It began officially on 26 June 1948, although it was not yet able to fulfil the huge requirements of Berlin over a long period. The pilots were enthusiastic and the organization makeshift. Smith divided his headquarters into two main sections: one for operations, the other for supply and maintenance. U.S.A.F.E. was to provide all other support.

End of Movie
Sergeant Perry A. Bowman, 16th Infantry, M Company, had watched a movie at the Titania Palace on Schlossstrasse When the film was over, he left the theater, only to find no street cars in Berlin running, no city lights, no people walking. A passing GI told Perry to report back to his unit. Back at Roosevelt Barracks, he was given a jeep and a Thompson submachine gun and ordered to man a post, in case of a Soviet attack. In the morning, replacement guards arrived and Sgt. Bowman was assigned to unloading incoming aircraft at Tempelhof.

Speed Trap
On 26 June 1948, after the U.S. military commanders had ordered strict speed limits within the city, Soviet Field Marshal Sokolowsky was caught speeding through the U.S. sector. Two MPs (military police) pulled the car over, but failed to recognize him. Neither could speak the other's language. The Field Marshal's guards arrived with guns raised. An MP placed a gun at Sokolowsky's stomach and demanded that they lower their weapons. The tense situation, came to an end, about an hour later, when a U.S. officer arrived and recognized Sokolowsky. He informed the Russian General he could proceed, but should obey the speed limit in the future.

Operation Plainfare
The British Army of the Rhine first inquired, at the Air Ministry Headquarters on 4 April 1948, into the possibility of supplying its forces in Berlin by air. By 25 June 1948, when the Soviet blockade began, **Operation Knicker** started to provide supplies (approximately 65–87 tons daily) from Wunstorf and Fassberg, using 16 Dakotas (Dakota was the R.A.F. designation for the C-47). The problem soon escalated: 2,016 tons of food would be required daily to maintain the German civilian population within the British sector. By 26 July 1948, the British began **Operation Paterson** which soon was renamed **Operation Plainfare.** This was done because the first name was that of a well-known British moving company, and the Soviets proclaimed this as an indication of a planned evacuation of Berlin.

The Headquarters of No. 46 Group, which commanded all R.A.F. and civilian-contracted aircraft, was in Lüneburg. The British managed the Airlift by direct subsidiary control at each airfield, through a Station Operations Control Room, which divided the tasks into four functions: aircrew control, servicing control, load control, and air traffic control.

Kit for Ten Days
The R.A.F. attempted to provide its aircrews with the best possible accommodation and food. This was not easy early in the Airlift. Reverend Donald Cawthray from R.A.F. Wunstorf came home to his wife stating: "There are a whole lot of transport planes coming in from England... the pilots will be sleeping in my church!" An aircrew restaurant was open 24 hours at each airfield, so that crews could always count on a hot meal. Bedding was handled on a hostel system, with bedding issued and returned. R.A.F. crews had been ordered to take "enough kit (food and supplies) for ten days," believing, like their American counterparts, that the Airlift would be of short duration.

Early Routine
Regulations called for a pilot not to fly more than two sorties within a 24-hour period and not to exceed 100 hours flying time in a 30-day period. The R.A.F. average turned out to be 70 hours flying time within the 30 days, and the U.S.A.F.E. soon adopted this standard for its pilots.

At first, each nation was expected to be responsible for maintaining its own sector, but the French involvement in Indo-China prevented their contribution of aircraft. Therefore, the flight operations would be provided by the American and British Air Forces, supporting 60% and 40% of the work load respectively. Both forces were to airlift as much as they could, with the aircraft at their disposal.

As the Airlift increased in size, the R.A.F. used several different aircraft, such as Short Sunderland flying boats, 40 Douglas (DC-3) Dakotas, 35 Avro Yorks, and 26 Handley Page Hastings. In addition, 22 private operators were drafted into service, under the direction of British European Airways, and these had a conglomeration of aircraft of various sizes, shapes, and specialization. As described on page 47, this required careful attention to scheduling, operational procedures, and crew discipline. But the R.A.F. aircraft had the advantage of the Eureka beacons and radar.

In contrast, the U.S.A.F.E. and General Tunner quickly realized that one standardized aircraft type was far more efficient in many ways (page 46).

... with Vittles and Plainfare

Coordination
The **Combined Airlift Task Force Headquarters** in Wiesbaden provided traffic flow into the Berlin airfields and coordinated the air traffic patterns. Procedures, principles of operation, and chain of command were thus maintained separately by the U.S. and British forces. The **Berlin Airlift Co-ordination Committee,** located in Frankfurt, established the supply requirements. Supplies to British bases were stored, graded, and checked by units of the Royal Airfield Supply Corps, becoming known as the **Rear Airlift Supply Organization (RASO).** At Gatow, supplies were unloaded and organized in a very similar manner by the **Forward Airfield Supply Organization (FASO).**

Milk Run
The Commander of U.S. Army, Berlin, Gen. Frank Howley, had anticipated an unpleasant situation and had ordered 117 tons of powdered milk and 65 tons of condensed milk to be stored in Berlin. The Soviets approached city officials, intending to gain political influence by offering milk for the children, but were surprised when turned down, not realizing that Howley was prepared for the situation.

Major General Clarence R. Huebner, commander of U.S. Army forces in Germany, called Howley on a non-secure telephone line and asked if reinforcements should be sent. Howley answered that he had two well-trained battalions and stated: "The situation is tense, but I've got it in hand and I think we'll be able to handle it ourselves."

First Operations at Gatow
Aircraft at Gatow were not to remain on the ground for more than 50 minutes. When an aircraft approached the ramp, a truck with German driver and loading workers began heading towards the aircraft. Once the aircraft parked and the engines stopped, the truck would back up, a somewhat tricky operation. When a vehicle was full, a replacement would soon take its place. Another truck would bring cargo to be airlifted out of Berlin. Every week the R.A.F. airlifted approximately 1,500 tons of goods out of Berlin; usually electrical products, books, toys, etc. The transport of finished goods was very important, considering that the Berlin blockade had cost 43,143 workers their jobs.

Because Gatow was located near Lake Havel, arriving coal was transported to old barges, which moved it to storage sheds within Berlin. This was the least expensive means (and most energy-efficient) of transporting the heavy cargo. The R.A.F. flew and managed the aircraft, while the RASO and FASO were responsible for ground handling.

> **Scrambled Egg**
> One pilot was amused, when he read the manifest; "two thousand miscellaneous electrical gears and two hundred pounds of scrambled egg" were to be airlifted out of Berlin. The "scrambled egg" referred to the gold braid found on high-ranking R.A.F. officers and as the officer was heavy, his weight had to be noted.

The French did not fly directly for the Airlift, but they provided vital support at Tegel, in the French Zone of Berlin (see page 35) and on occasion displayed some splendid Gallic gallantry (see page 73).

Lieut-General Curtis E. LeMay, Commander-in-Chief, U.S.A.F.E.

General Sir Brian Robertson, British Military Governor and Commander-in-Chief, Germany.

The Berlin Airlift did not have the luxury of electronic or computerized systems, and most of the planning was done the old-fashioned way. Here, two officers of the British Royal Army Service Corps (R.A.S.C.) discuss problems of delivery and storage of supplies at Gatow—on the blackboard.

The First Airlifters: Dakota . . .
R.A.F. Douglas C-47

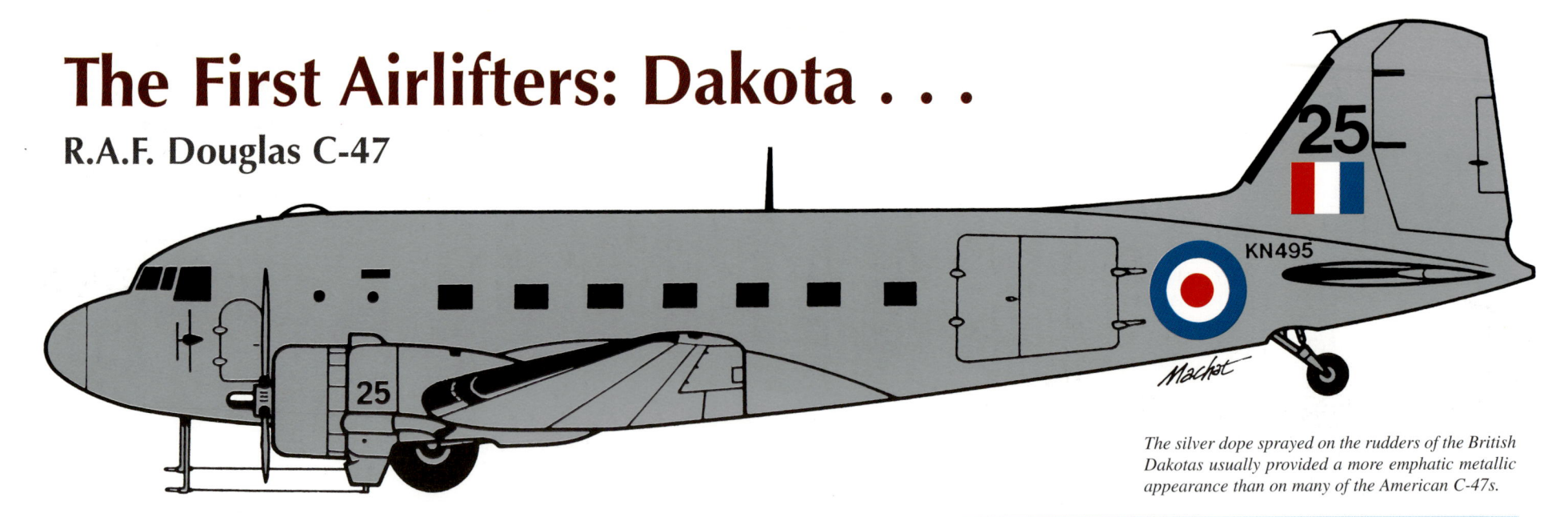

The silver dope sprayed on the rudders of the British Dakotas usually provided a more emphatic metallic appearance than on many of the American C-47s.

Payload 7,480 lb. ■ Speed 150 mph ■ Pratt & Whitney R.1830 Twin Wasp (1,200 hp) x 2 ■ Max. Gross Take-off Weight 31,000 lb. ■ Range 600 st. miles ■ Span 95 feet ■ Length 65 feet ■ Height 17 feet
Note: Standard commercial (civilian) max. Gross Take-off Weight was 26,000 lb., standard payload was 6,000 lb.

When, as early as April 1948, Soviet restrictions on surface travel from western Germany to Berlin began to make themselves felt, the thrice-weekly R.A.F. Avro Anson flights from Bückeburg were replaced by **Douglas Dakotas,** and frequency grew to thrice-daily. But these were employed solely to supply the British troops in Berlin.

But as the restrictions intensified, the Dakota fleet was increased, with 16 of these reliable and by now veteran transport aircraft assigned to the main R.A.F. base at Wunstorf. As **Operation Knicker** got under way, these were carrying 65 tons of freight per day, the R.A.F. having increased the normal C-47 payload from 5,500 lb. to 6,500 lb. by removing unnecessary internal fittings and decreasing the required range and thus reducing the fuel load.

The R.A.S.C. troops stationed in Berlin for Operation Knicker were excused speed limit restrictions so that they could comply with the urgency of the task. One soldier, entering into the spirit of such urgency, obtained (according to a carefully worded official account) "from an undisclosed source, a garment corresponding to the codename, and hung it as a pennant from the window of his car." Presumably this gave him swift access to the road to the airport, rather as priority is given to a general's pennant.

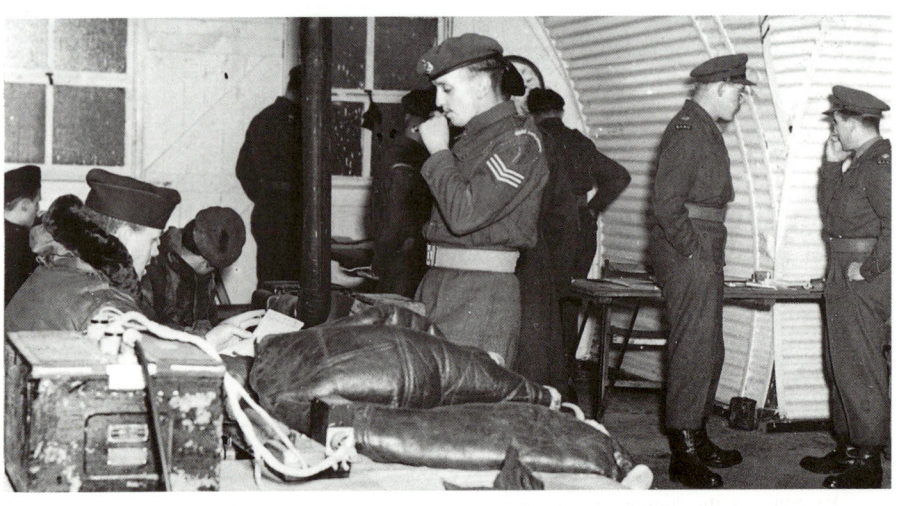

The Royal Army Service Corps (R.A.S.C.) and the Royal Engineers of the British Army provided a substantial element of the ground service personnel at all the air bases in the British sector. Their often improvised quarters were relatively primitive in Nissen (Quonset) huts. In this photograph, a British sergeant discusses a local problem with an American colleague. (U.S. Army Signal Corps)

... and Skytrain
U.S.A.F. Douglas C-47

Payload 7,480 lb. ■ **Speed 150 mph** ■ **Pratt & Whitney R.1830 Twin Wasp (1,200 hp) x 2** ■ **Max. Gross Take-off Weight 31,000 lb.** ■ **Range 600 st. miles** ■ **Span 95 feet** ■ **Length 65 feet** ■ **Height 17 feet**
Note: Standard commercial (civilian) max. Gross Take-off Weight was 26,000 lb., standard payload was 6,000 lb.

Douglas C-47 Skytrain, nicknamed *Gooney Bird*
Developed from the pioneering DC-1/DC-2, the **Douglas DC-3** became one of the most successful commercial airliners in history. Starting service with American Airlines on 25 June 1936, it dominated air transport in the U.S.A. until the end of the Second World War. 10,926 were built in the U.S., mostly as **C-47s** or other military variants during the War. Only 433 were original DC-3s and only a few of the earliest were DSTs (Douglas Sleeper Transports) which were at first specified by the launch customer. More than 4,000 were built at the Douglas plant at Long Beach, and more than 6,000 at Oklahoma City and Chicago. Under license agreements, 487 more were built in Japan, and 6,157 in the Soviet Union, as Lisunov Li-2s, of which production continued for a few years at Tashkent during the post-war years.

Grass-Strip Versatility
The DC-3/C-47 could be relied upon to land or take off from grass or otherwise 'unprepared' airstrips, and was thus especially versatile for Berlin Airlift work until the airfields in west Germany and Berlin could be improved by the hasty construction of paved runways, able to accept the movements of the heavier four-engined Douglas C-54s.

Evidence of the adaptability of the veteran Douglas airliner can still be found all over the world, where they provide a variety of transport services, mainly for freight, but occasionally even for passengers. Their longevity has been phenomenal.

A panoramic view of Rhein-Main AB at Frankfurt shows some C-54s and the austere airfield service accommodations—mobile offices, tents, and one of the improvised maintenance docks. (Gloria Wenk)

General William Tunner

General Tunner Arrives
Generals Clay, LeMay, and Smith were combat commanders but an airlift specialist was required to make the Berlin Airlift a success. The U.S.A.F. Chief of Staff, General Hoyt Vandenberg, sent **Lieutenant General William H. Tunner** to take over command of the operations.

Willie-the-Whip
In the summer of 1944, Tunner had assumed command of what became known as The Hump. This operation had started in April 1942, with the Tenth Air Force, a combat unit, transporting supplies from 13 air bases in India to 6 bases in China, across the Himalaya mountains, a formidable obstacle. By December 1942, the Tenth was relieved and the Air Transport Command placed in charge. The 23,000 tons of supplies airlifted per month were not sufficient for the China Theater. The accident rate was high and morale was low. Pilots used to say that they did not need a map to find the proper route, they would simply watch for the wrecks below. But by July 1945, one year after Tunner arrived, the tonnage had increased to 71,000 per month, boosting morale; and the accident rate was improved. Tunner's hard-won experience, compiled over many months, enabled him to tackle the Berlin Airlift, with a large number of aircraft, crews, and personnel, to transport a huge amount of material, almost overnight. His insistence on strict discipline earned him the nickname: Willie-the-Whip.

The Old China Hands
To ensure success, Tunner called upon many of his former Hump personnel, including Col. Red Forman who would became chief of operations; Maj. Edward A. Guilbert, director of traffic; Lt.Col. Orval O. McMahon; Col. Kenneth E. Swallwell, director of Air Installations; and Lt.Col. Manuel 'Pete' Fernandez, communications officer. New to the group, Col. Theodore Ross Milton would become chief of staff; and 1st Lt. William G. Thompson would become public information officer and editor of the newspaper *Task Force Times*. In all, General Tunner hand picked his staff of twenty officers and they started work on 29 July 1948.

During the initial organizing of operations, many problems arose. Tunner's staff immediately made a quick tour of bases and operations to learn the situation. They discovered poor flight and maintenance scheduling, lack of coordination, and general confusion. The serious problems of this cowboy operation became apparent at Tempelhof on Friday, 13 August 1948, better known as Black Friday.

Black Friday
On that day: "the clouds dropped to the tops of the apartment buildings surrounding the field, and then they suddenly gave way in a cloudburst that obscured the runway from the tower. The radio could not penetrate the sheets of rain. Apparently both the tower operators and the ground-control operators lost control of the situation. One C-54 overshot the runway, crashed into a ditch at the end of the field, and caught fire; the crew got out alive. Another Skymaster, coming in with a maximum load of coal, landed too far down the runway. To avoid piling into the fire ahead, the pilot had to brake with all he had; the tires blew. Another pilot, coming in over the housetops, saw what seemed to be a runway and let down. He discovered, too late, that he had picked an auxiliary runway that was still under construction, and he slithered and slipped on the slick surface for several precarious moments, then groundlooped."

General Tunner's track record in airlift operations was impeccable. During the Second World War he supervised the India-China 'Hump' supply route, hailed as an impressive aviation achievement.

General Tunner had much experience with military airlift operations. The son of Austrian emigrants, he graduated from West Point in 1928. During the Second World War, he helped to organize the Army Air Corps Ferrying Command, which grew to 50,000 military and civilian personnel. It carried out more than 291,000 missions and delivered 21,000 aircraft to foreign destinations. Tunner is seen here with his deputy, British Air Commodore J.W.F. Merer (see page 30).

With all that confusion on the ground, the unloaded aircraft ready for takeoff had to wait for fear of collision with the planes 'stacked up' above. The incoming aircraft had no place to land and were slowly running low on fuel. Tunner, who was in an airplane heading for Berlin, ordered all aircraft to return to their home bases. Within four days, twenty crack Civil Aeronautics Authority air controllers from Oakland, La Guardia, and Chicago were ordered back to duty as reservists and on their way to Germany. The tragedy of Black Friday was never repeated.

BEALCOM

BEALCOM

The **Berlin Airlift Co-ordination Committee (BEALCOM)** became responsible for obtaining products in the required quantities and transporting them to the different air bases. It met twice monthly and was part of the **Bipartite Control Office (BICO)**; both located in Frankfurt. At the predetermined bases, the R.A.F. or U.S.A.F.E. was responsible for the loading of each aircraft and the flight operations. In Berlin, they were divided among the three military powers. Tempelhof (U.S. sector) provided for the U.S. and French military; Tegel (French sector) provided for all three; and Gatow (British sector) supplied the British military. Most of the supplies from all three bases were given to a German official, the Magistrat of Berlin, who then distributed them.

Building an Aerial Armada

At the beginning, the 60th and 61st Troop Carrier Groups were ordered to fly the maximum number of missions to Berlin. By 30 June 1948, 102 C-47 Skytrains (DC-3s, nicknamed Gooney Birds), were assigned to the Airlift, with each capable of transporting an average of only about 3 tons. The Airlift Task Force determined the daily requirement to support Berlin to be 4,500 tons per day. The C-47s, with their small load capacity, could not fulfil this requirement. The larger C-54s (DC-4s) first appeared in July 1948 and by 1 January 1949, 200 U.S.A.F. and 24 Navy C-54 aircraft were operating in the Airlift. The small C-47s were totally replaced by 1 October 1948. As many as 240 C-54s operated in the U.S. Airlift, with 100 more in the maintenance pipeline or reconditioning depots. On the British side, 40 C-47 Dakotas, 35 Avro Yorks, and 26 Handley Page Hastings were deployed.

During the closing weeks of the Airlift, the Boeing C-97 Stratofreighter (see page 28) arrived for trials. These larger and better equipped cargo aircraft could carry at least 20 tons each, and had the Airlift continued, would no doubt have been impressed into service in large numbers—and emphasized to the Soviets the massive logistics capability of the western Allies.

The C-54s replaced the smaller C-47s and were soon operating in large numbers. One is seen here unloading a cargo of wood for constructing temporary buildings. (Gloria Wenk)

The C-54s, with tricycle landing gear, provided a level surface for loading and unloading. (Robert Pine)

Royal Air Force C-47 Dakotas at Gatow. As with the C-47 Skytrains of the U.S.A.F., these were soon supplemented with larger aircraft. (U.S.A.F.)

The Corridors

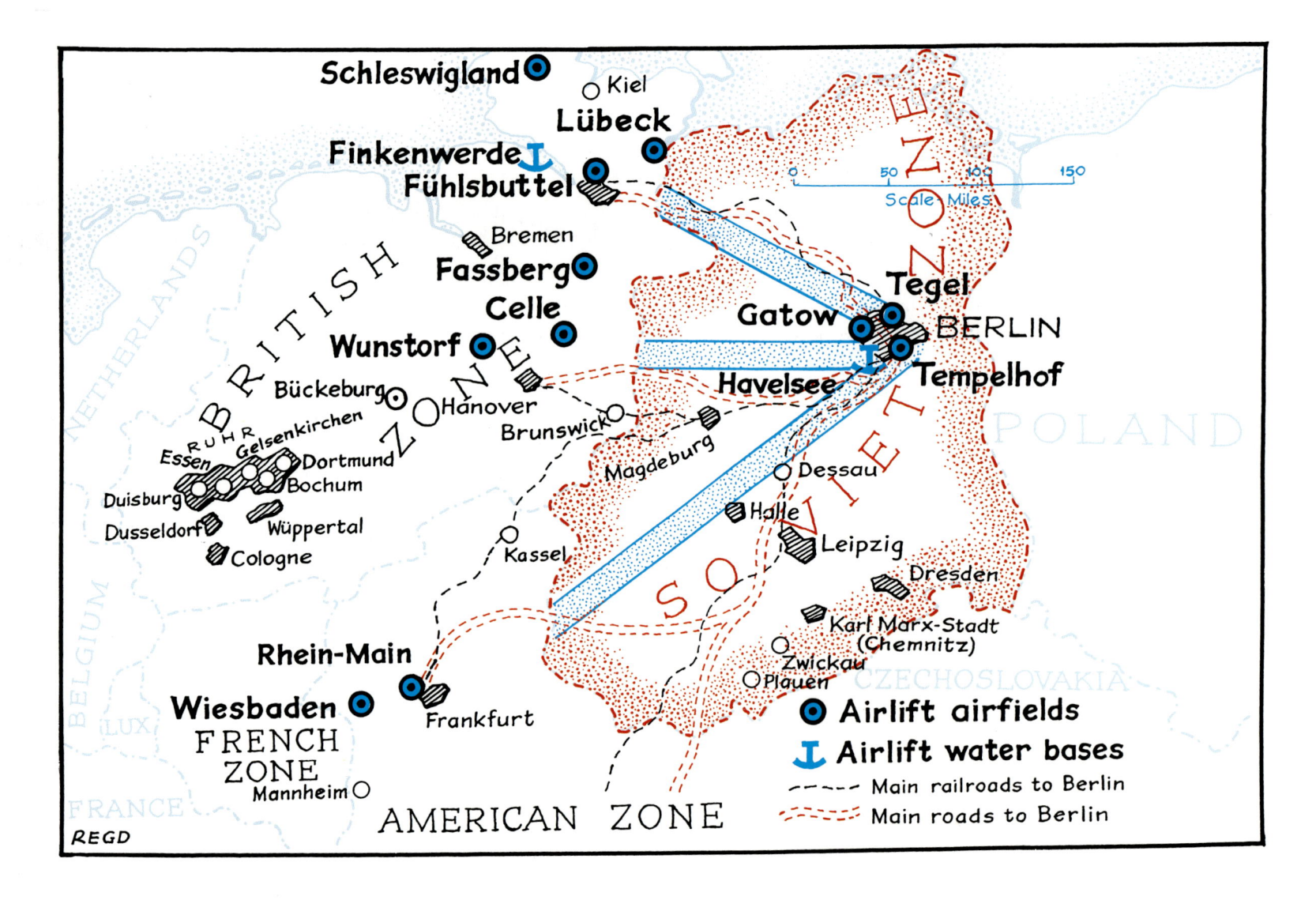

Douglas C-54G Skymaster

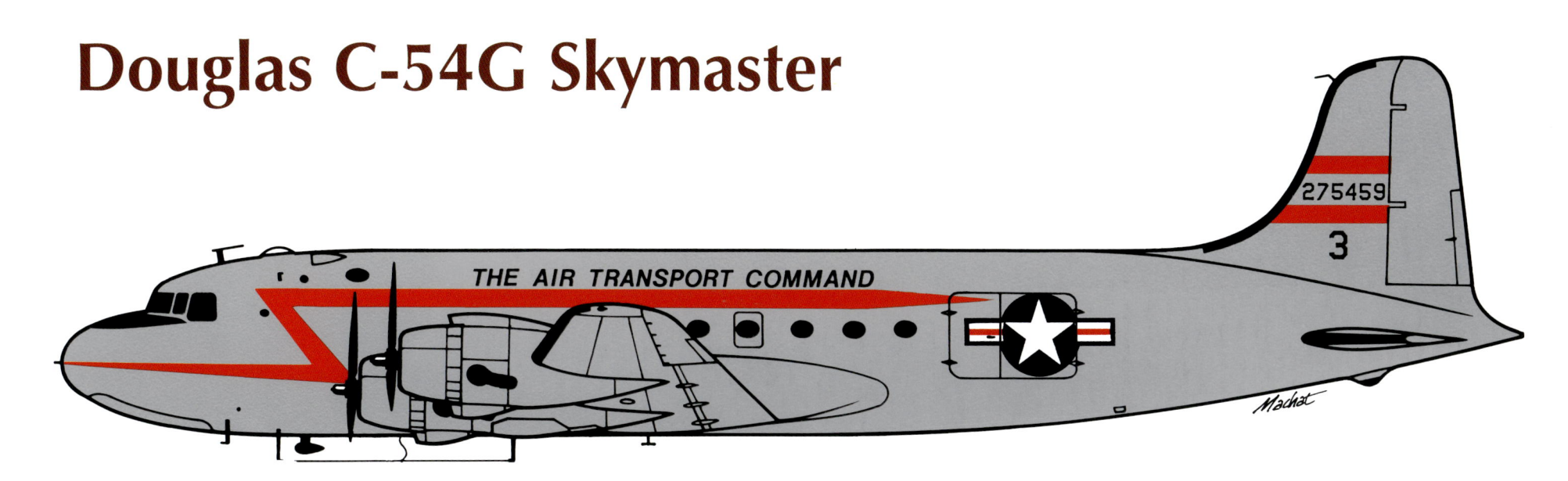

Payload 19,500 lb. ■ **Speed 170 mph** ■ **Pratt & Whitney R-2000 (1,450 hp) x 4** ■ **Max. Gross Take-off Weight 73,000 lb.** ■ **Range 1,200 st. miles** ■ **Span 117 feet** ■ **Length 94 feet** ■ **Height 28 feet**
Note: For the short-range Airlift operations, the payload was often exceeded, up to 22,000 lb. or more.

The C-54 Skymaster was the workhorse of the Airlift, carrying an unprecedented volume of material that hitherto had not been considered suitable for transporting by air. More than 300 of these fine aircraft were placed into service, and, as described elsewhere in this book, carried enormous tonnages of coal and food supplies.

Skymaster . . .

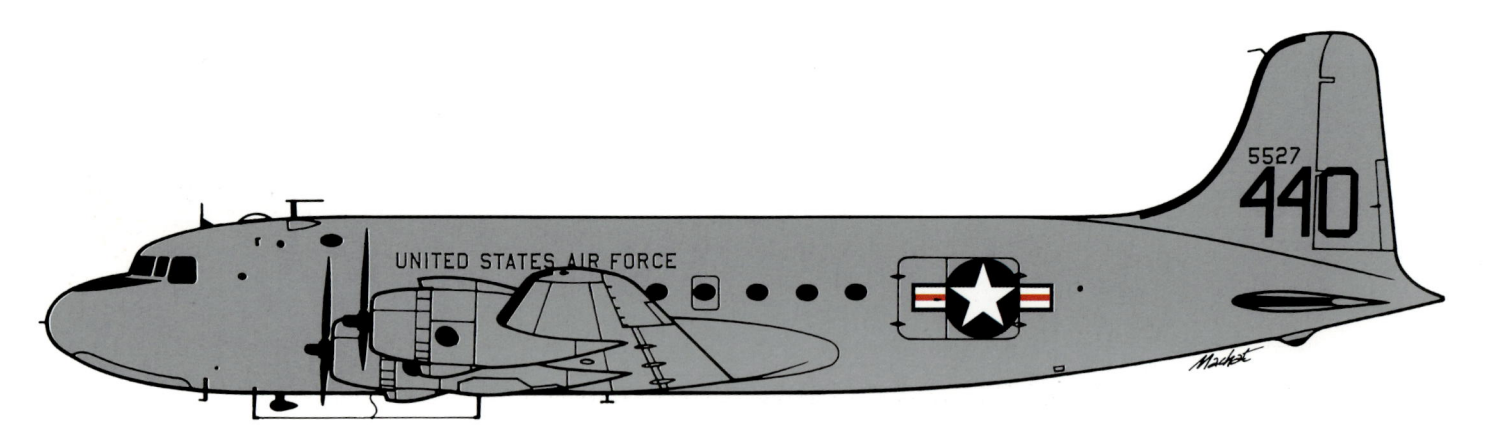

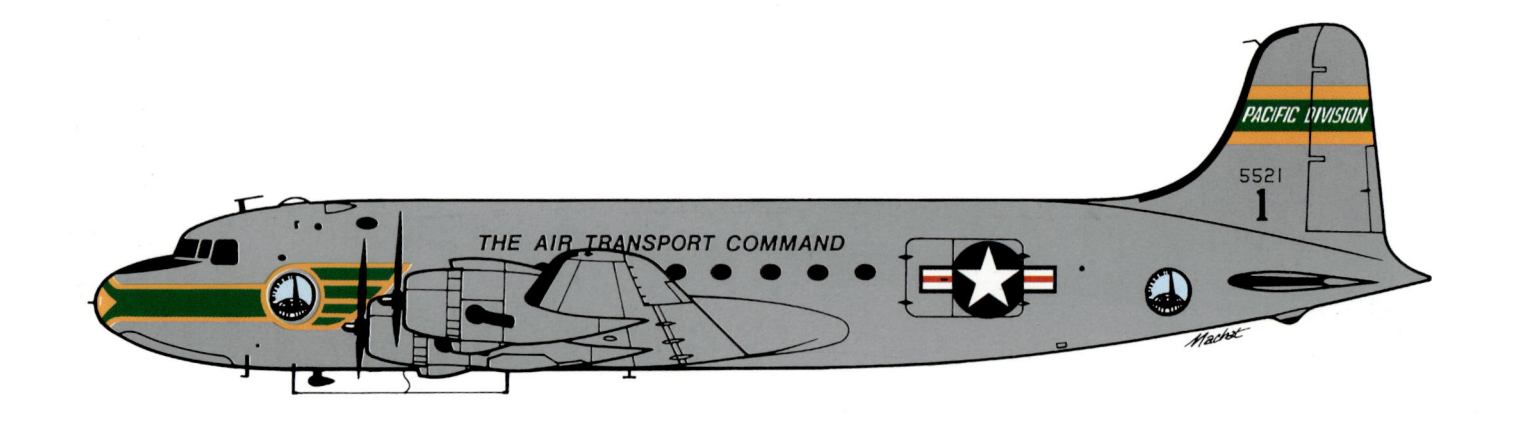

Douglas C-54 Skymaster
The DC-4 was developed as a civilian passenger aircraft, but by the time it made its maiden flight on 14 February 1942, the world was at war and the full production was devoted to the military C-54 version. The United States military ordered 1,163 of these aircraft. Powered by 4 Pratt & Whitney R-2000 Twin Wasp (1,450 hp) engines, it had a maximum gross take-off weight of 73,000 lb., a payload of 19,500 lb., a maximum speed of 274 mph, and a range of 2,500 miles—enough to cross the world's oceans.

... Master of the Berlin Skies

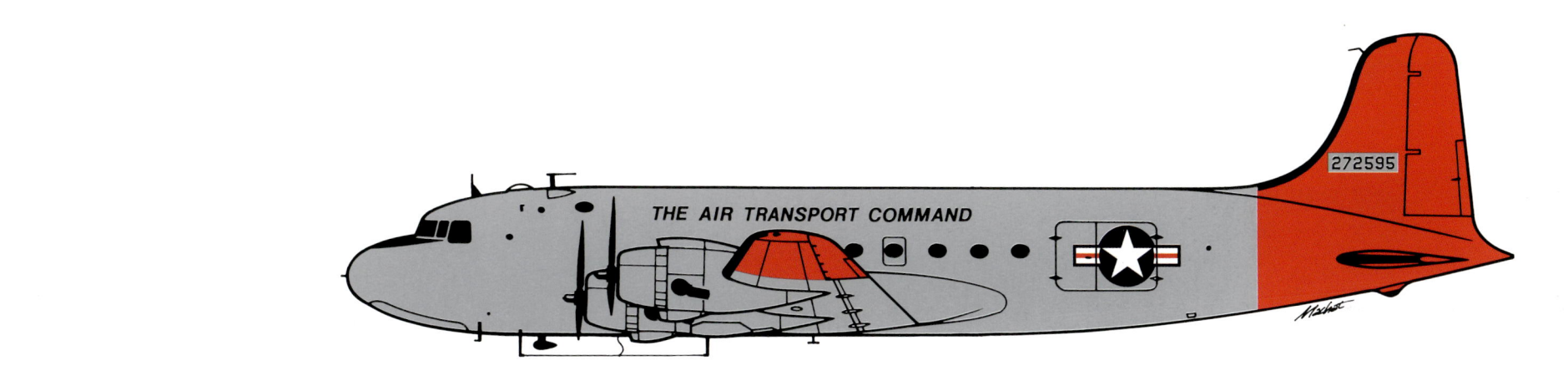

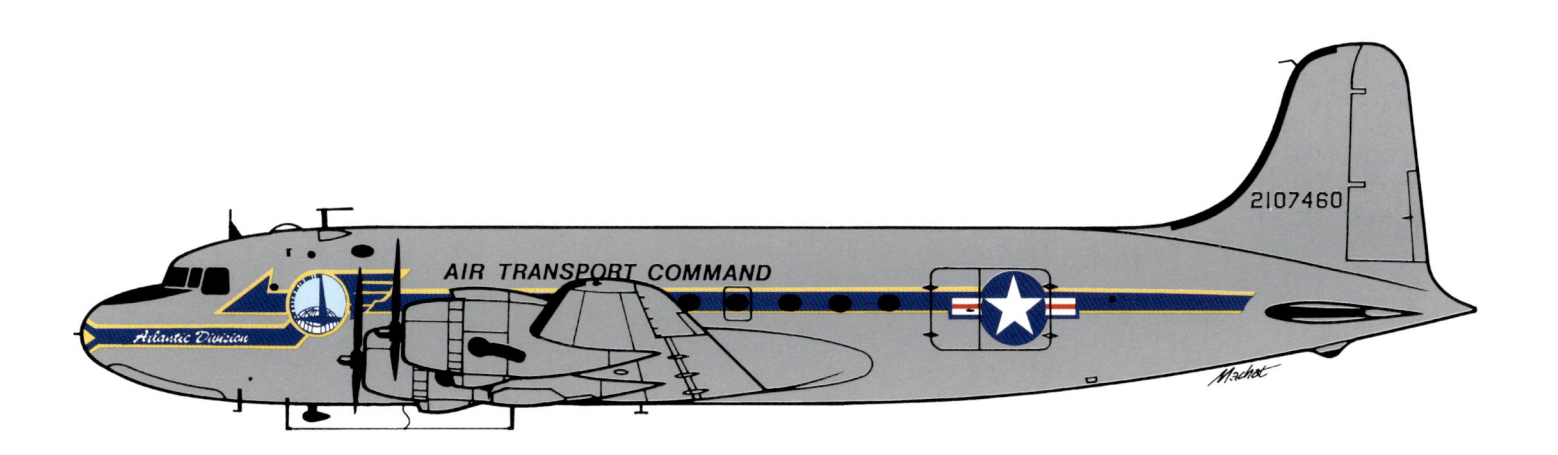

Artist's Note
The Douglas C-54 Skymaster presents a particular challenge to the artist, because the airplane began its career with the U.S. Army Air Corps during World War II, served with the newborn U.S. Air Force during the Berlin Airlift, and went on to support the Military Air Transport Service in both the Korean and Vietnam conflicts. During the time of the Berlin Airlift, the C-54 appeared in a whole range of color schemes, from olive drab camouflage to the airliner-type liveries of the late 1940s (as shown on the dust jacket), and even unpainted, with only the U.S. national insignia adorning its bare metal skin. The markings shown here are a representative sampling of the many 'uniforms' worn by the C-54.

Douglas C-74 Globemaster I

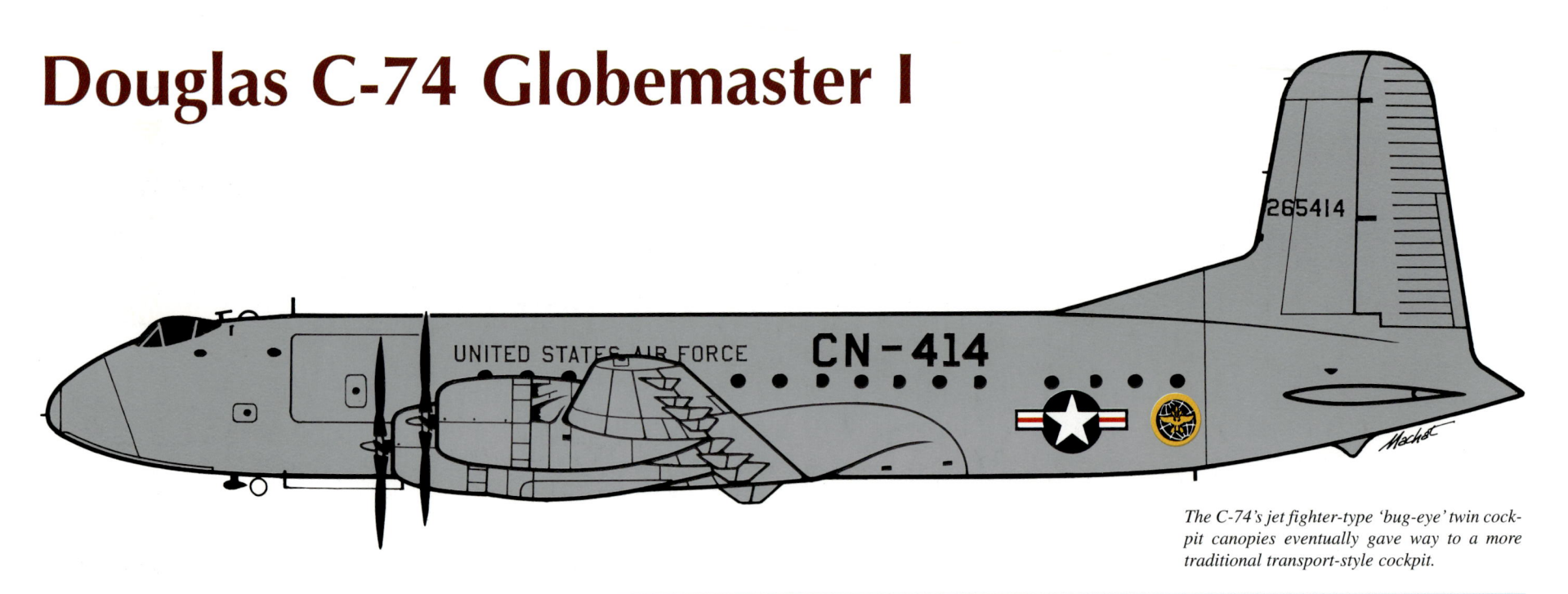

The C-74's jet fighter-type 'bug-eye' twin cockpit canopies eventually gave way to a more traditional transport-style cockpit.

Payload 48,000 lb. ■ Speed 185 mph ■ Pratt & Whitney R-4360-49 (3,500 hp) x 4 ■ Max. Gross Take-off Weight 172,000 lb. ■ Range 1,500 st. miles ■ Span 173 feet ■ Length 124 feet ■ Height 44 feet

One C-74 became available early during the Airlift. It arrived on 14 August 1948 and was later used to carry Pratt & Whitney engines from the U.S. to the C-54s in Germany. It made 25 flights and carried 446 tons.

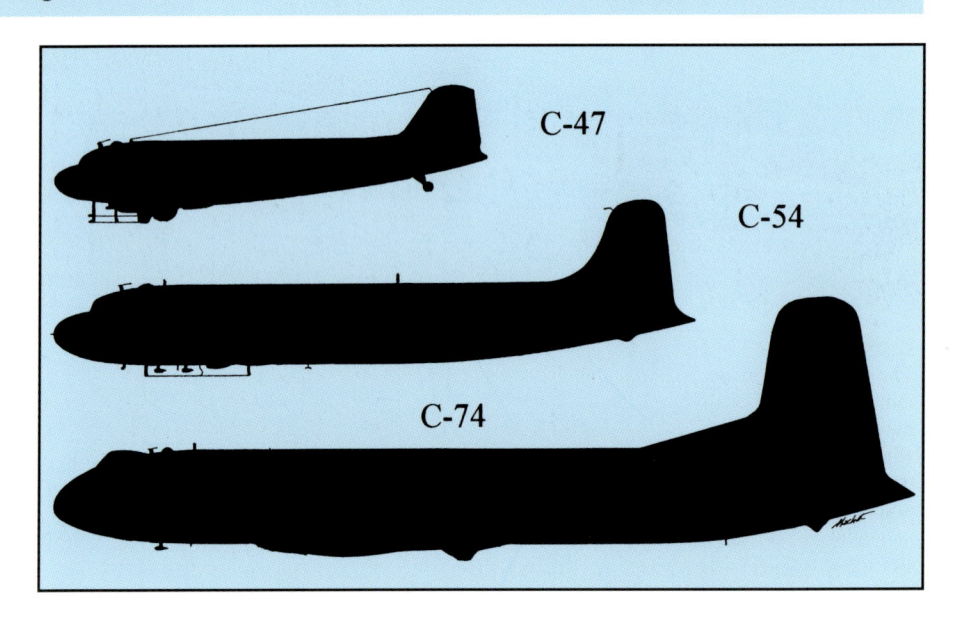

26

Fairchild C-82 Packet

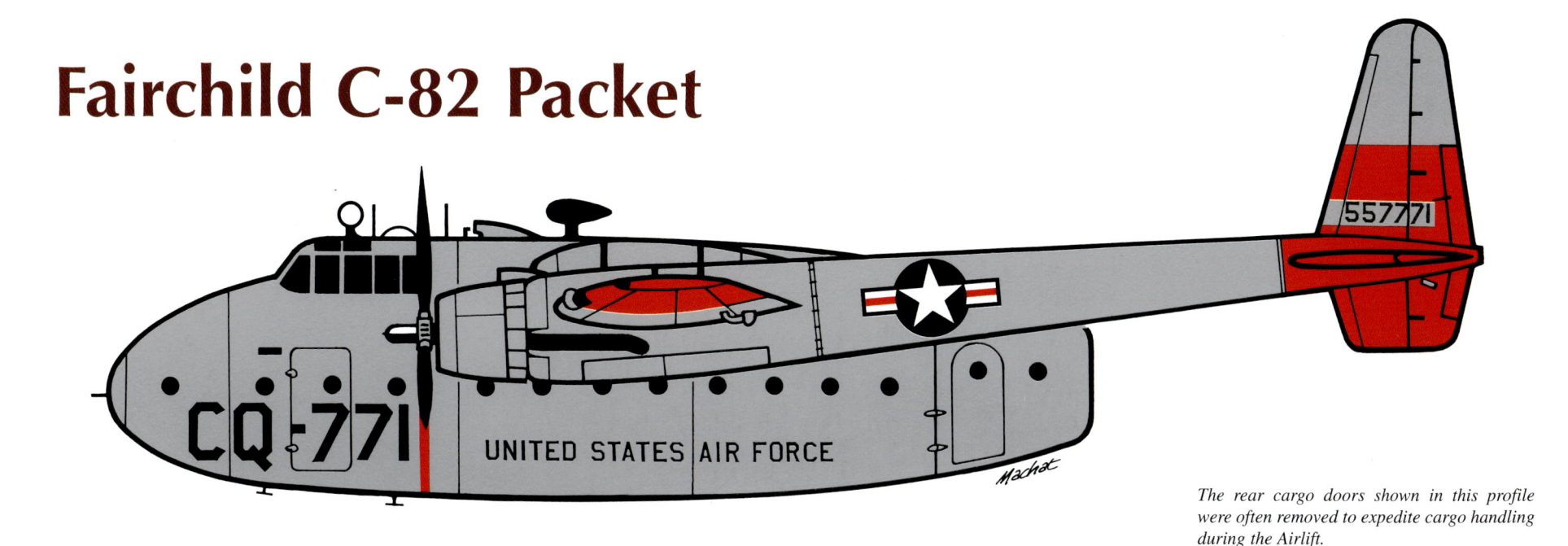

The rear cargo doors shown in this profile were often removed to expedite cargo handling during the Airlift.

Payload 12,000 lb. ■ Speed 170 mph ■ Pratt & Whitney R-2800-85 (2,100 hp) x 2 ■ Max. Gross Take-off Weight 54,000 lb. ■ Range 500 st. miles ■ Span 107 feet ■ Length 77 feet ■ Height 26 feet

(U.S.A.F.)

Fairchild C-82 Packet

The C-82 first flew on 10 September 1944, but deliveries began late in 1945 and ended in September 1948. A total of 223 Packets were built. On 13 September 1948, a unit of 5 C-82s, commanded by Capt. George A. Kemper, arrived at Wiesbaden A.B. and was later assigned to Rhein-Main A.B.. The C-82 transported vehicles, graders, snowplows, ambulances, and jeeps to Berlin. They also airlifted parts for the new electric power station then under construction, and other large items.

The famous C-119 Flying Boxcar was developed from the C-82, and more than 1,100 of this improved variant were built.

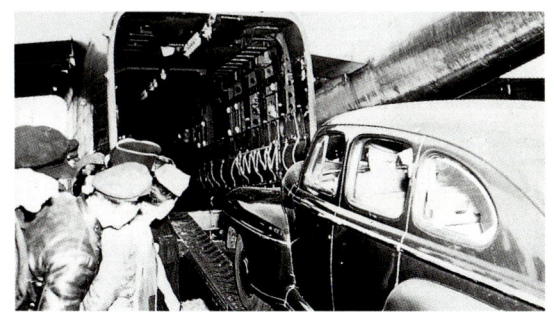

Although only a small part of the total Airlift fleet, the Packet came with its own ramps, and was especially useful for large loads such as these. (U.S. Army Signal Corps)

Boeing C-97 Stratofreighter

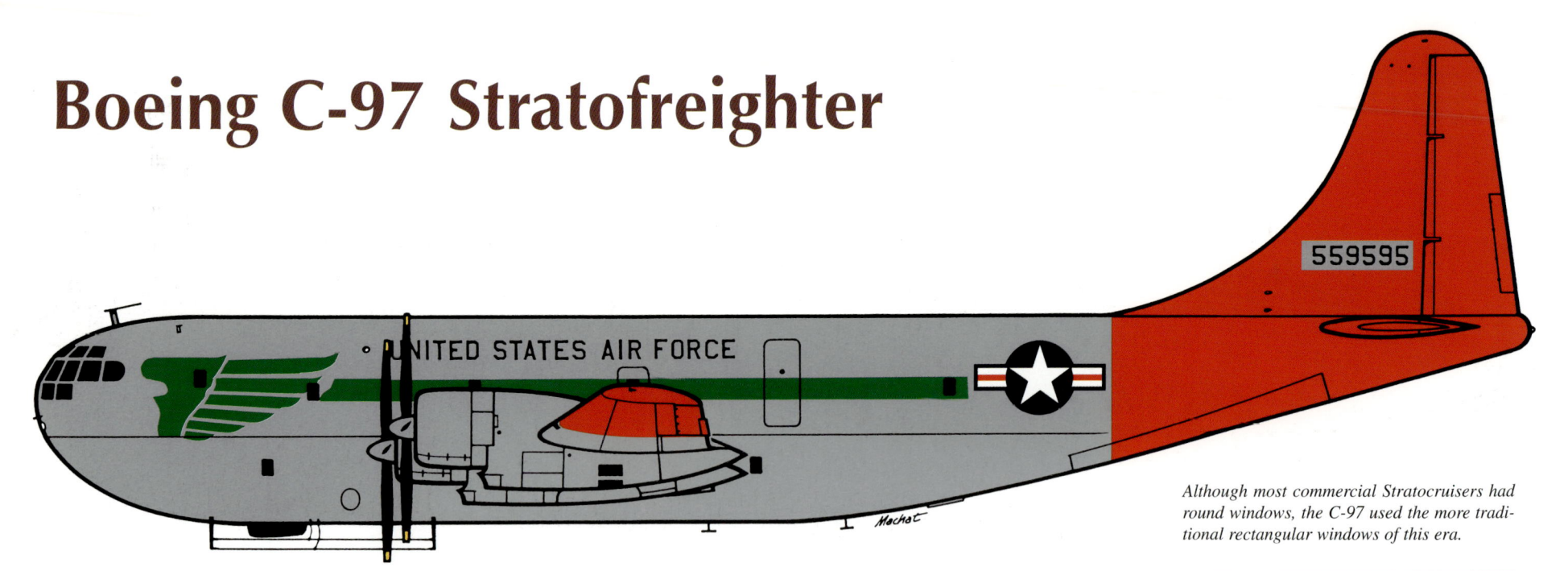

Although most commercial Stratocruisers had round windows, the C-97 used the more traditional rectangular windows of this era.

Payload 53,000 lb. ■ Speed 200 mph ■ Pratt & Whitney R-4360-27 Double Wasp (3,500 hp) x 4 ■ Max. Gross Take-off Weight 142,500 lb. ■ Range 1,500 st. miles ■ Span 141 feet ■ Length 110 feet ■ Height 33 feet

Although the first C-97 arrived at Rhein-Main on 3 May 1949, only a few days before the blockade ended, it did play a part, psychologically as well as practically. It operated into Berlin from 4 to 9 May, with Boeing service engineers monitoring the movements and loads. These latter totalled 20 tons for most of the flights, either coal, dehydrated potatoes, or rice. Its reversible-thrust propellers enabled it to stop only two-thirds of the distance down the Tempelhof runway. On the last flight into Berlin, General Tunner was on board, and was no doubt impressed. Had the Airlift continued, 52 Stratofreighters could have carried the same load into Berlin as 240 C-54s—and additional aircraft had been ordered for the U.S. Air Force. No doubt this must have impressed the Soviet observers too—for different reasons. (U.S.A.F.)

Douglas R5D (Naval C-54)

Except for minor details (such as the antenna, engine exhausts, and propellers, the Navy R5D was the same as the Air Force C-54 (see page 23 for performance, specification, and dimensions).

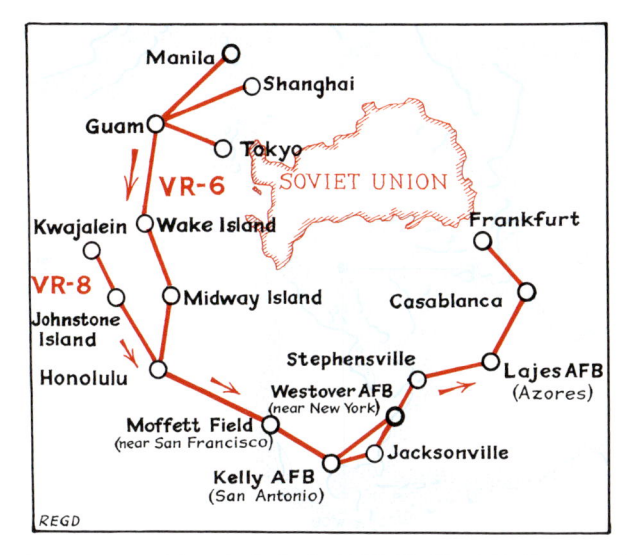

The Navy came a long way to participate in the Berlin Airlift. The **Naval Air Transport Service (NATS)** had two squadrons based in the Pacific. **VR-6** was serving the western Pacific as far as China and Japan; and **VR-8** was deployed mainly in the west central islands. Orders were received on 27 October 1948 and 20 R5Ds left on 1 November from Honolulu's John Rogers Field. These were augmented at Moffett Field to the full strength of 24 for the two squadrons. They were fitted with radar at Jacksonville, but unfortunately this was not compatible with the system at Tempelhof, Berlin. The Navy, as narrated on page 68, was to excel itself in a climate far different from the tropical Pacific sun.

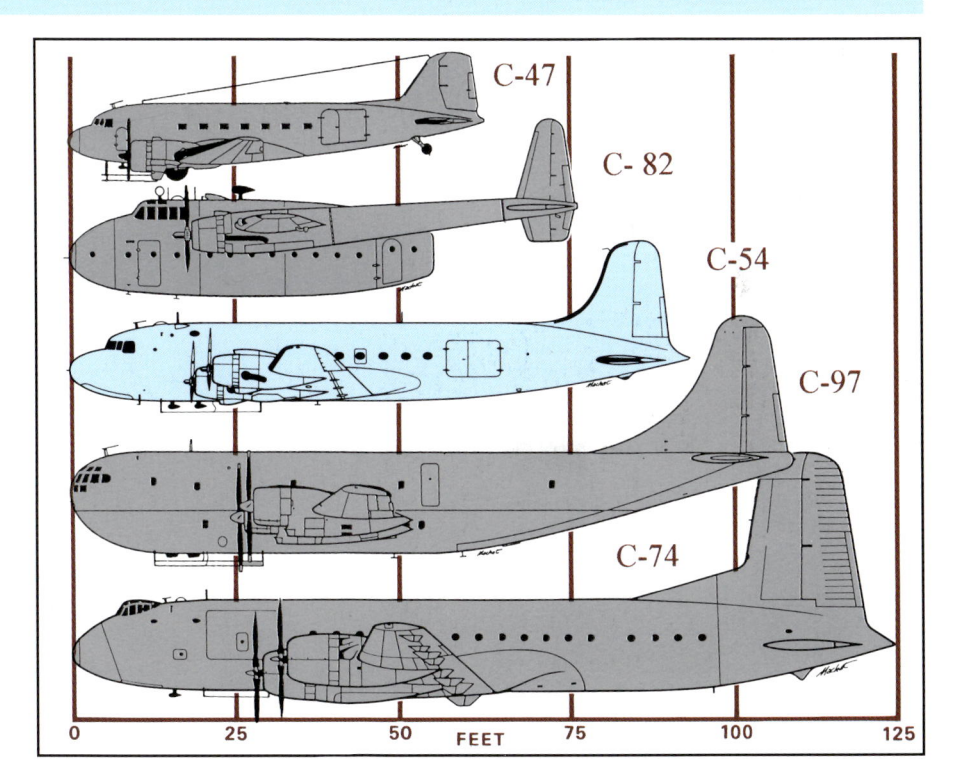

Getting Under Way

Reinforcements
With Turner's arrival, **MATS (the Military Air Transport Service),** which provided military air transport around the world, supplied U.S.A.F.E. with the aircraft and personnel required for the Airlift. On 23 July, just a few days before Tunner's arrival in Germany, 682 Officers, 1,818 airmen and 20 civilians transferred to Germany as part of the MATS support of the Airlift, which included several squadrons of C-54s. General LeMay was promoted and replaced as Commander-in-Chief, U.S.A.F.E. three months after Tunner's arrival by **Lieutenant General John K. Cannon.**

Build-Up
Operation Vittles was divided into two periods. The first two months of operation saw the extensive use of the C-47. With limited load capacity, it was nevertheless the only aircraft available in Europe in large numbers. By August, 1948, C-54s comprised half of the aircraft flying and by October the C-47s had been totally replaced. The C-54s reached their maximum strength of 240 aircraft (which included 24 Navy R5Ds) by 15 January 1949.

The early days of the Airlift were filled with hustle and bustle, and good reports of increased tonnage. General Tunner said, "the actual operation of a successful airlift is about as glamorous as drops of water on stone. There's no frenzy, no flap, just the inexorable process of getting the job done." The U.S.A.F. realized this, so Tunner was placed in command of the Berlin Airlift Task Force (Provisional) on 1 August 1948.

The C.A.L.T.F.
His headquarters were at Taunus Strasse 11, Wiesbaden, later known as the **Composite Airlift Task Force (C.A.L.T.F.).** It was officially created on 15 October 1948. The British **Air Commodore J.W.F. Merer** was assigned as deputy, although he spent much of his time with the R.A.F. Group No. 46 in Lüneburg. The R.A.F. and U.S.A.F.E. were operating large numbers of aircraft in a restricted air space. A combined headquarters was imperative.

In the early weeks the operation was unable to increase tonnage. When Tunner arrived, he assessed the situation: "We look upon the Lift not as an end in itself. It is an exercise in the technique of using big airplanes in a manner hitherto unknown." Tunner believed that certain factors: immaculate maintenance, safety, instrument flying, rhythm, radar-assisted approaches, and competition—all these were vital for the success of the Airlift.

> "In a successful airlift you don't see planes parked all over the place; they're either in the air, on loading or unloading ramps, or being worked on. You don't see personnel milling around; flying crews are either flying, or resting up, so that they can fly again tomorrow. Ground crews are either working on their assigned planes, or resting..." (General Tunner)

Aircraft were drawn from all possible sources within the U.S. Armed Forces.

Code Name	No. of C-54s	From	Dates*
Able	45	Alaskan Air Command Troop Carrier Command	28 June–11 July 1948
Baker	9	MATS, Continental Division	10–13 July 1948
Charlie	72	MATS Atlantic Division, 2 Squadrons Pacific Division, 4 Squadrons Continental Division, 2 Squadrons	23 July–16 Aug. 1948
Dog	36	FEAF (Far Eastern Air Force)	10 Sept.–10 Oct. 1948
Easy	24	MATS, 2 Naval Squadrons	27 Oct.–11 Nov. 1948
Fox	10	MATS, AWS Pacific Division	9 Nov.–16 Dec. 1948
George	20	MATS, AMS, TAC Continental Air Command	12 Nov. 48–12 Jan. 1949
How	24	MATS, AACS	17 Nov. 48–10 Jan. 1949
Total	**240**		**28 June 48–12 Jan. 1949**

* The dates given are the days required to fly the aircraft to Germany, from the first day of departure to the last day of arrival in each group.

The C-54 of the U.S.A.F. was the main element that ensured the success of the Berlin Airlift. Operating a fleet of the same aircraft simplified the availability of spare parts and trained crews; and also ensured operational commonality in performance and navigating procedures.

British Commonwealth Support

British Commonwealth Support

The **R.A.F.**'s Operation Plainfare began at Wunstorf, while civilian carriers at first operated from Buckeburg to Gatow. Aircraft from Wunstorf transferred to Fassberg on 29 July 1948, while civilian carriers moved to Wunstorf. On 21 August, the R.A.F. moved again from Fassberg to Lübeck, to provide space for the arriving U.S. C-54s. A **Royal Australian Air Force** Squadron, with twelve complete crews, joined the Airlift in October. South Africa dispatched ten crews of No. 3 Squadron, **Royal South African Air Force** on 22/23 September 1948, under the command of Maj. D.M. van der Kaay. This contingent was supported by South Africans serving in No. 24 Commonwealth Squadron R.A.F., and rotated in April 1949, being replaced by a second group of pilots.

Like their American colleagues, they suddenly left family and friends behind, leaving Pretoria to arrive at Oakington, England, on the 26th. These units arrived at Lübeck on 18 October and occupied comfortable former Luftwaffe quarters. The next day, they began flying in the Airlift and continued until the final afternoon of 5 April 1949. The R.S.A.A.F. flew 2,500 sorties and delivered 8,333 tons. Overcrowding forced a transfer of aircraft from Lübeck to Fühlsbuttel. The story for the R.A.A.F was similar. In November, the **Royal New Zealand Air Force** arrived with three complete crews. These Commonwealth crews, which comprised a pilot, navigator and wireless operator, flew R.A.F. Dakotas continuously until the end of the Airlift.

A Mixed Fleet

A major problem for the British was the use of several different aircraft types. The Americans replaced their C-47 aircraft with up to 240 C-54 aircraft early during the Airlift, standardizing on one type of aircraft that could maintain a sustained closely scheduled operation. The use of different aircraft, with varying performance and speeds, greatly handicapped the British. Different air speeds meant variations in altitude and complex air traffic patterns. The R.A.F. adopted a policy of sending different types out in groups or streams, with the slower aircraft going first.

Versatility

Some aircraft, such as the Hastings, had a landing gear that could not be used in a 20-knot crosswind. The U.S. C-54 could still operate with a 35-knot crosswind. On the other hand, the British aircraft, in their very variety, could provide specialized capacity. While the American C-54s and R5Ds carried all the coal, dehydrated or powdered potatoes (more economical than in their natural form) and most of the flour for the 'staff of life': bread, the Lancastrians and Halifax/Haltons carried all the liquid fuel. Indeed, the 'Lancs' of Flight Refuelling were already adapted for that very purpose. The hulls of R.A.F. Sunderlands were already anodized as protection against sea water, and were therefore ideal for carrying the corrosive salt. Later when the flying boats could not alight on Lake Havel, some of the Halifaxes were also anodized to resist corrosion.

A Handley Page Halifax of Skyflight, one of the 23 British commercial companies drafted into service for the emergency. The underside of the fuselage was fitted with a removable pannier (where the bomb bay used to be) for ease of loading. (E.J. Riding)

An Avro Lancastrian, of Flight Refuelling, one of the companies chartered by the British government. Specially designed for in-flight refuelling of other aircraft to provide increased range, this type was already equipped to carry fuel. (The A.J. Jackson collection)

Combined Airlift Route Pattern

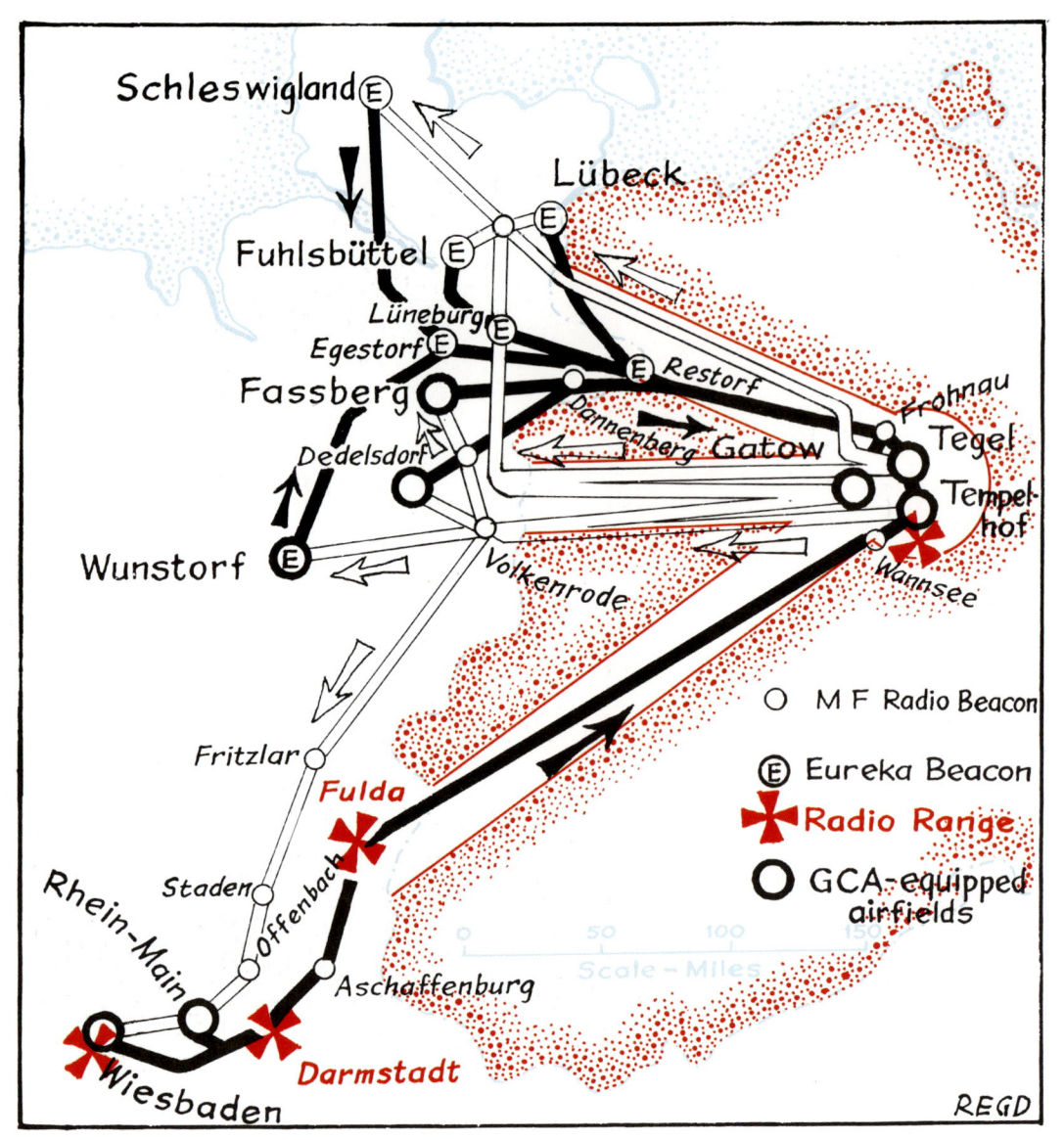

This map illustrates the Standard Operating Procedures of the Combined Airlift Task Force.

The Traffic System
The three air corridors into Berlin were 20 miles wide, and pilots had to take great care not to stray away from them. Of the three aerial avenues, two were strictly one way, to cope with the American C-54s streaming into and out of Tempelhof Airport at the rate of one every three minutes at peak times. The northernmost corridor was two-directional, but as far as the limitations of corridor width allowed, the Berlin-bound aircraft tended to keep to the southern edge of the corridor, while the westbound British aircraft, often carrying passengers, kept to the north.

The Beacons
The British aircraft flying the northern and central corridors were aided by **medium-frequency (M/F) radio beacons** and **Eureka radar beacons** for navigational guidance. The M/F beacons sent out continuous signals, activating the navigators' radio-compasses, while the Eureka beacon responded to impulses from the aircraft's Rebecca Set, and, on a radar screen, showed the bearing and distance from the beacon.

The most frequently used beacon was at Frohnau, at the northern approach to Berlin. Inevitably it became known as the Fräulein.

Radio Ranges
The southern (Berlin-bound) corridor had **Radio Range beacons,** a system developed with great success in the United States as early as 1930. 'A (• —)' or 'N (— •)' signals (of the morse code) in alternate quadrants became a continuous note when the aircraft were exactly at the line of coincidence.

Ground Controlled Approach
The busiest airfields were equipped with the **Ground Controlled Approach (G.C.A.)** system. Developed by the U.S. Air Force, this displayed, on a radar screen at the airfield, the height, bearing, and distance of all aircraft within 40 miles. The Ground Controller could thus direct all aircraft by radio exactly how to approach and land. Without G.C.A., the Berlin Airlift could never have attained the intensive scheduling necessary to accomplish its mission.

Ultimate Destination: Berlin's Tempelhof Airport
(Smithsonian Institution)

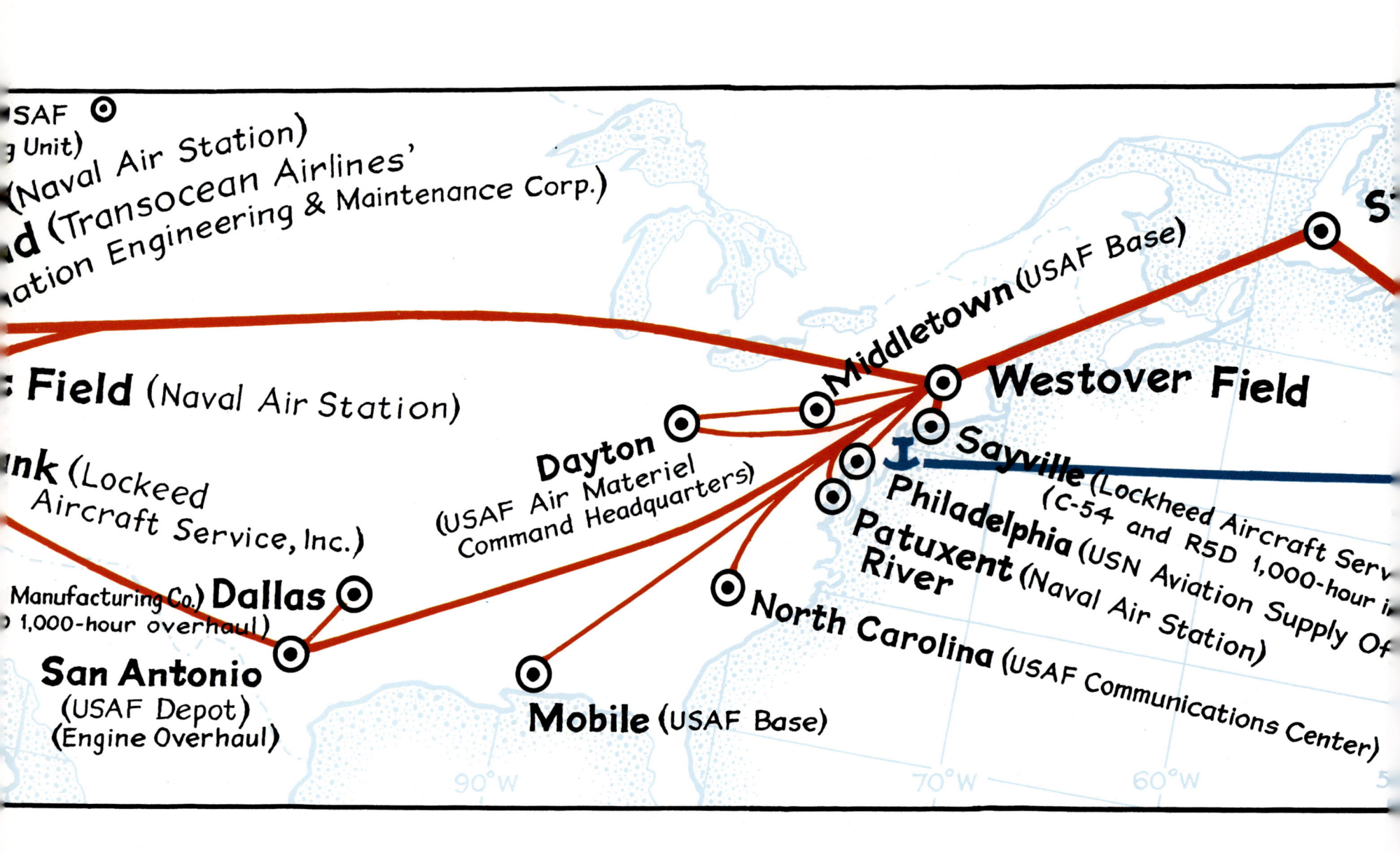

...SAF ⊙
...g Unit)
...(Naval Air Station)
...(Transocean Airlines'
...ation Engineering & Maintenance Corp.)

Field (Naval Air Station)

...nk (Lockeed
...Aircraft Service, Inc.)

Manufacturing Co.) **Dallas** ⊙
1,000-hour overhaul)

San Antonio
(USAF Depot)
(Engine Overhaul)

⊙ **Dayton**
(USAF Air Materiel
Command Headquarters)

⊙ **Middletown** (USAF Base)

⊙ **Westover Field**

⊙ **Sayville**
(Lockheed Aircraft Serv
C-54 and R5D 1,000-hour i

⊙ **Philadelphia** (USN Aviation Supply Of

⊙ **Patuxent River** (Naval Air Station)

⊙ **North Carolina** (USAF Communications Center)

⊙ **Mobile** (USAF Base)

The Airlift Aerial Coal-Trucks:
Nine C-54s load up in line at Frankfurt, while a tenth aircraft awaits its turn.
A few C-47s, a Beech C-45, and a B-17 are in the background. *(John Provan collection)*

The full extent of the complex logistics of the Berlin Airlift is often overlooked. While the concentration of effort was within Germany, much of the precious cargo came from across the Atlantic. Also, the aircraft had to return periodically to authorized maintenance bases, one of them as far away as Tranocean Airlines' fine engineering installation at Oakland, California. All flights had to stop at Lajes airfield, on Terceira Island, in the Azores, as the C-54s did not have non-stop trans-Atlantic range.

Adaptability:
The British charter companies drew upon a motley assortment of aircraft—but they did the job.

Consolidated Liberator of Scottish Airlines. *(Provan)*

Avro Tudor 5 of B.S.A.A. **(specially equipped to carry diesel fuel).** *(Provan)*

Short Sunderland of the Royal Air Force (specially treated to carry salt). *(Provan)*

Handley Page Halifax of the Lancashire Aircraft Corporation (with detachable pannier, or pod, underneath the fuselage). *(Jackson)*

The supply lines for the British element of the Airlift were short. Aircraft could fly in from England, from various airfields, directly to the Airlift terminals in the British Zone of Germany.

The trans-Atlantic sea route was also an important contributor to the Airlift. Little more than three years previously, Allied ships had been avoiding U-Boats; they now carried supplies to the former German capital, which had become a beleaguered city.

Final Approach: A C-54 comes in to land at Tempelhof
(Smithsonian Institution)

phenville

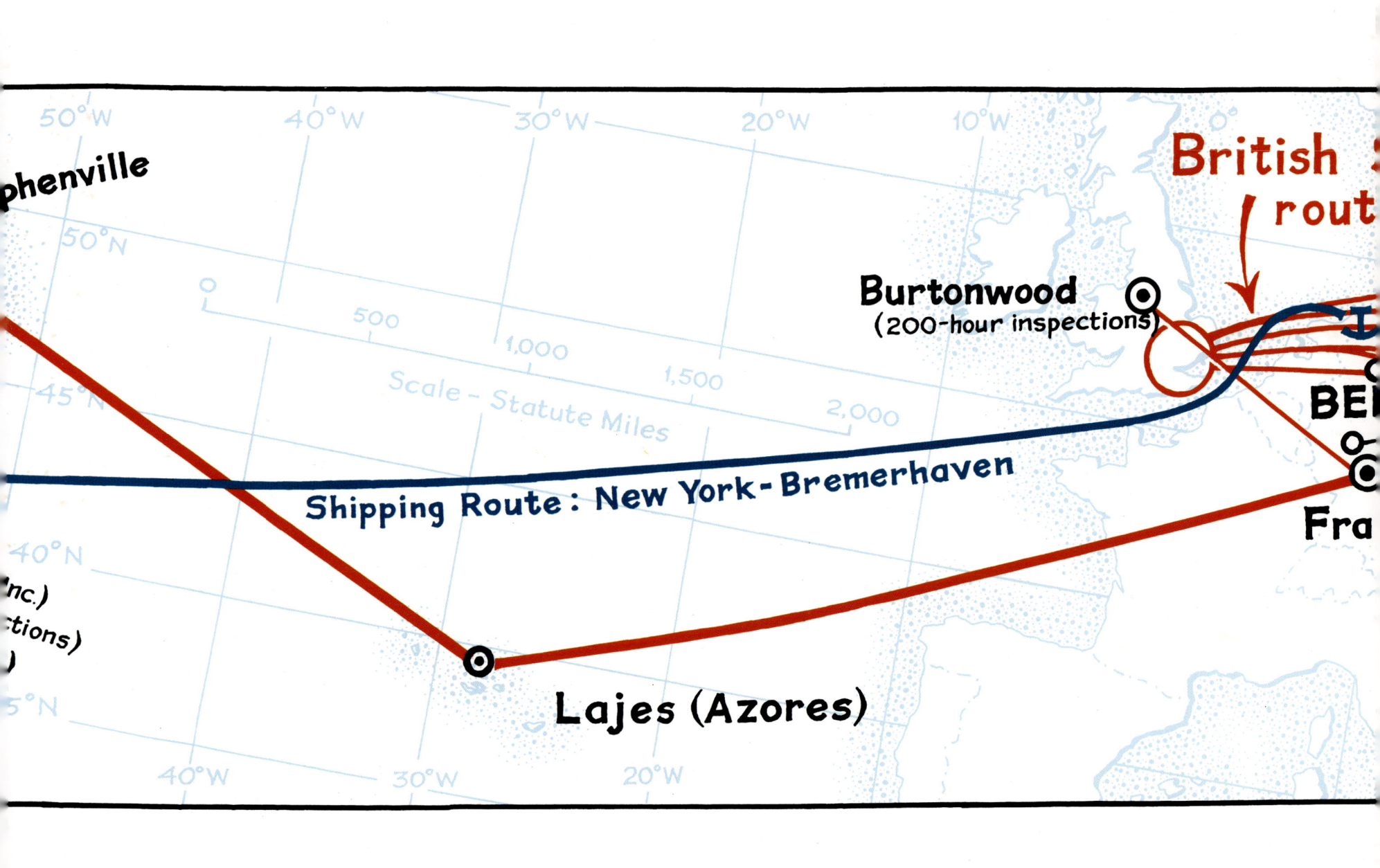

Burtonwood
(200-hour inspections)

British
rout

Shipping Route: New York-Bremerhaven

Lajes (Azores)

The Berlin Approaches

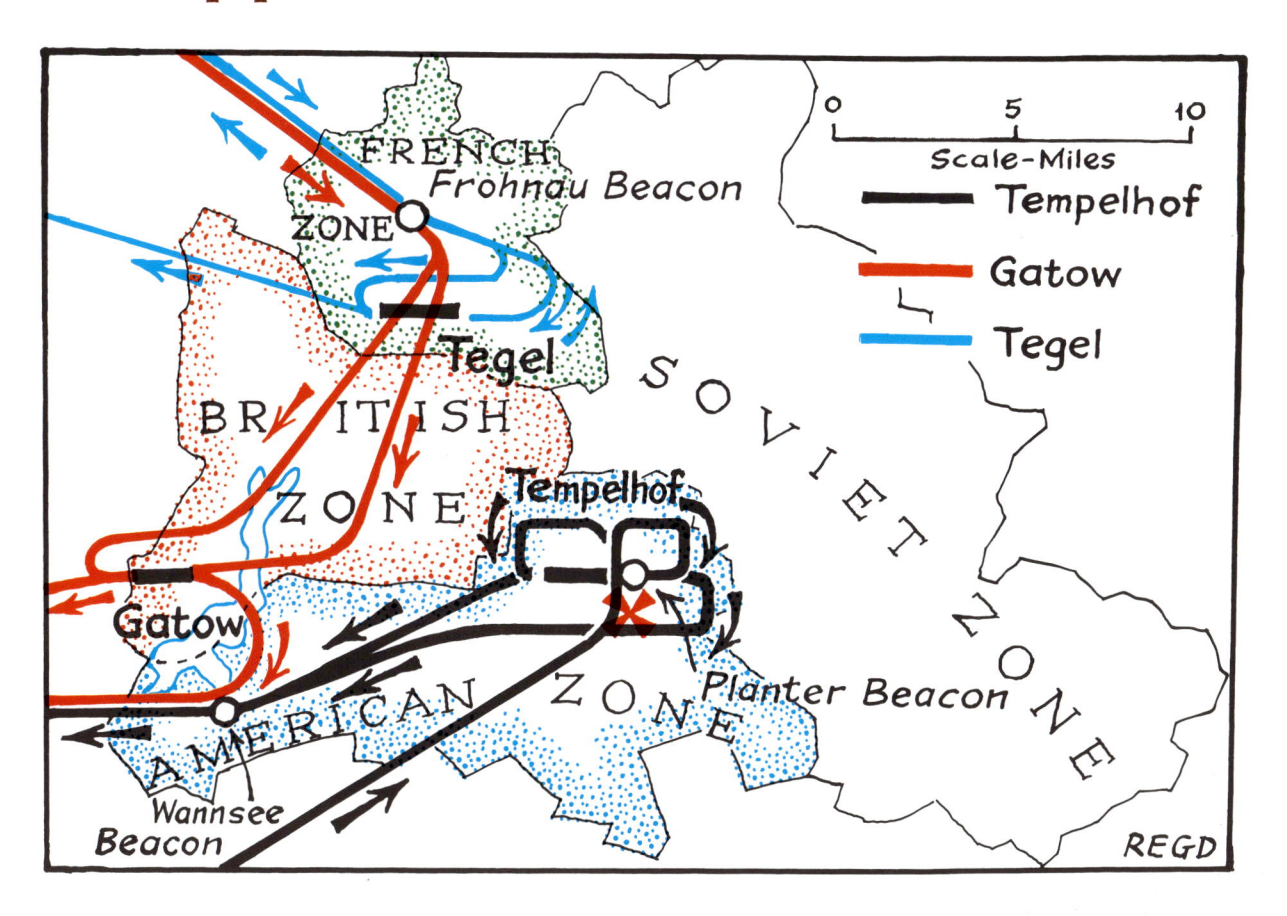

A Crowded Airspace
The Berlin Airlift quickly became a crowded series of aerial highways. The density of traffic and aircraft movements, with frequency intervals often at the rate of 20 per hour or more, demanded strict discipline in airfield landing and approach procedures. This was accentuated when the increasing demand led to a third airport, Tegel, in the French Zone, being quickly improved to greater runway strength.

Special Procedures
The proximity of the Soviet Sector of Berlin and of the Soviet Zone of eastern Germany imposed a handicap, forcing all aircraft to make some tight turns before landing. The congestion within the Allied sectors itself was no mean problem either.

Included in the Standard Operating Procedures for the Combined Airlift Task Force in the Berlin Area were such instructions as (at Tegel airfield): "Gatow-bound aircraft hold 2000' until past Tegel;" or "All missed approaches will follow departure procedures", i.e. the aircraft could not 'go round again' but had to return to base, otherwise confusion, or worse, would have arisen.

Landmarks
The Berlin Airlift crews soon became used to the routine, demanding though it was of stamina, tolerance, and patience. The routes became familiar. The Frohnau (referred to as the 'Fräulein') Beacon was a familiar radio landmark, and the red-lighted Kaiser Wilhelm I memorial soon became 'The Christmas Tree.' At Gatow, the area where the coal was unloaded inevitably became 'Newcastle'—reflecting the familiar association in the British mind of the city identified with that commodity. The map illustrates the routes taken over Berlin, and emphasizes the proximity to the Soviet Zone.

Berlin — Tempelhof

Tempelhof

Tempelhof was built as an imposing city airport for Berlin. Designed by Prof. Dr. Sagebiel, it was constructed between 1934 and 1940, but was only 70% complete by the end of the war. Although the Russians burned some installations, most of the structure was still standing when the U.S. Army's 301st Troop Carrier Squadron arrived and established it as an Air Base on 2 July 1945. The 473rd Air Service Group was responsible for the initial cleanup of the ruins and some essential reconstruction. Colonel Booth, the first Commander of Tempelhof A.B., organized facilities and began improvements.

Runway Construction

Tempelhof did not have a paved runway before the war, only a paved ramp area. The 862nd Engineer Aviation Battalion constructed the first east-west (central) runway, completed during the Airlift. The second (southern) runway was built between 6 July and 12 September 1948, while a third runway was built between 6 and 28 October, 1948.

Tempelhof's terminal building is almost one mile in length, greatly assisting the Airlift in providing 3.1 million square feet of surface space. American Overseas Airlines maintained normal commercial operations between Rhein-Main A.B. and Tempelhof A.B. during the Airlift.

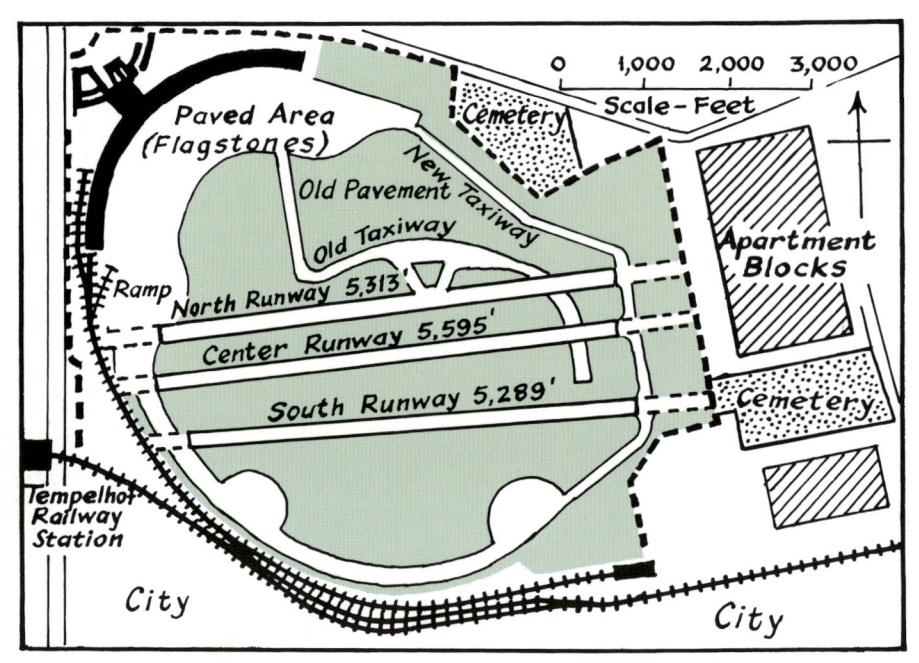

This aerial view, from the west, clearly shows the almost mile-long airport buildings that were so impressive. The picture also shows the over-run extensions of the central runway. The picture was taken in September 1948, before the third runway was built. (U.S.A.F.)

This map clearly shows the position of the notorious cemetery at the eastern end of the south runway, serving as a cautionary note against landing short, or getting too close to the apartments.

The apartment buildings that surrounded Tempelhof Airport were as much of a hazard as the cemetery, especially in conditions of poor visibility on the approach. The residents did not complain too much about noise.

Berlin — Gatow and Tegel

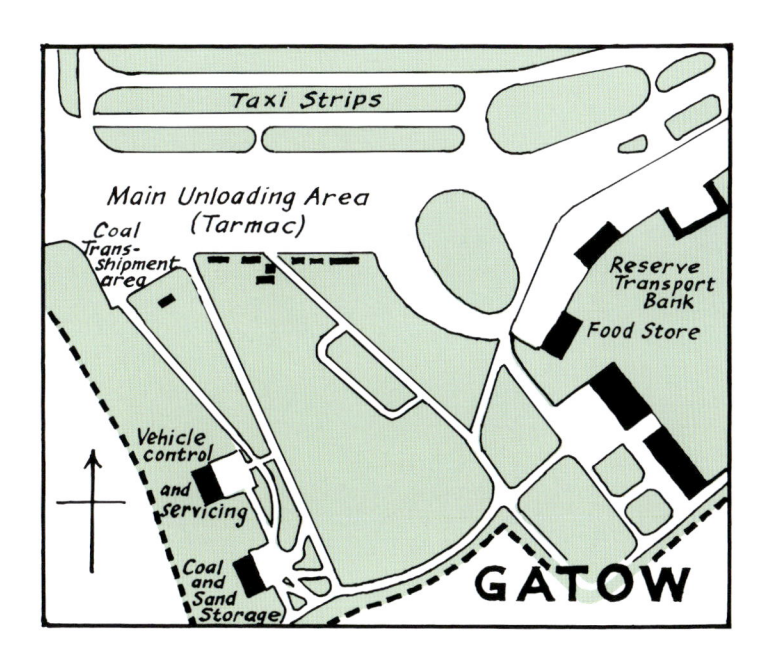

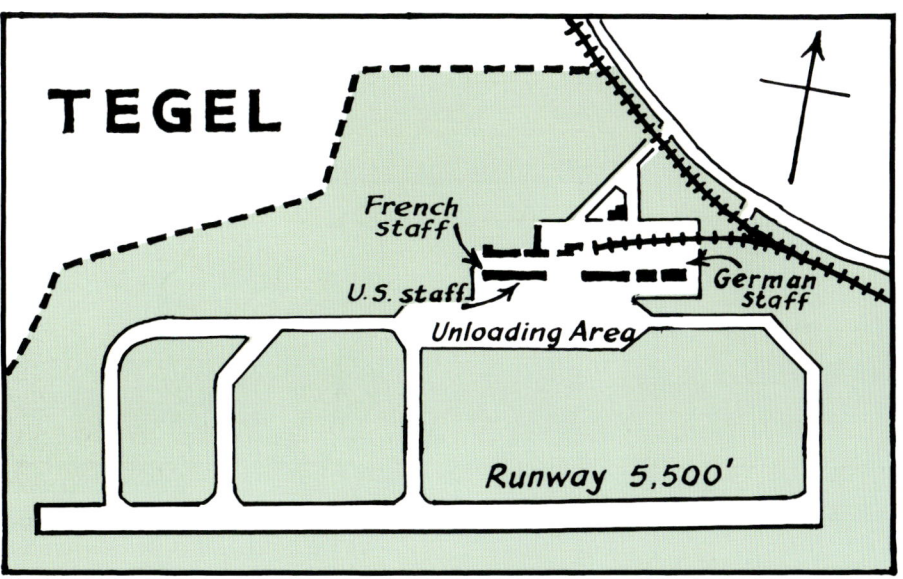

Gatow
R.A.F. Station Gatow was built in 1936 by the German Luftwaffe. The Base was well equipped with hangars, offices, and barracks, which had survived the war without damage. The R.A.F. built a P.S.P. (Pierced Steel Planking) runway in 1946. A concrete runway was under construction when the Airlift began and completed on 17 July 1948. The paved apron was built from more than 14,000 tons of rubble. Some earth work was started on a second runway, before the Airlift ended, but stopped after the blockade ended as it was no longer required. The U.S. military began using Gatow in August, to relieve congestion at Tempelhof. Station Commander was Group Captain B. Yarde. About half of the tonnage of all Airlift freight into Berlin was handled through Gatow—twice as much tonnage as at Tempelhof and three times as much as at La Guardia Airport in New York.

Tegel
During the Airlift another airfield was required in Berlin. Tegel, in the French sector, was a former airship training base, used during the Great War of 1914-18. During the Second World War, it was used to train German anti-aircraft units.

Thousands of Berliners built the foundation without any heavy equipment, using rubble from the war-damaged city. Between July and October 1948, the runways, ramps, and most airport buildings were completed. Heavy equipment, such as bulldozers, rock crushers, and steam rollers, could not fit into the aircraft, requiring that all items be cut into smaller pieces. Once transported, the pieces were welded together and construction at Tegel A.B. was completed. The first R.A.F. plane, KN 446, piloted by A.M. Johnstone, landed on 18 October and discovered that the base was not quite ready. With no one to unload receiving aircraft, Johnstone brought his load back to Lübeck. The base formally opened in ceremonies on 15 December.

Tegel was disliked by pilots. It had neither G.C.A. (Ground Control Approach) nor BABS (Blind Approach Beacon System) and the control tower was inoperative. There was no direct telephone to the Berlin Air Safety Center, and there were few amenities. As time passed, the situation improved, with the majority of supplies arriving from Fassberg, or from R.A.F. Schleswigland and Fuhlsbüttel. The French Air Force handled all cargo and managed the civilian work force while the U.S.A.F. handled flying operations.

A Royal Air Force Avro York at Tegel.

35

The Southern Corridor Fields

Rhein-Main

Originally known as the Flug- und Luftschiffhafen (Air and Airship station) Rhein-Main, Frankfurt, this airport was built between 1934 and 1936, and was used by the Luftwaffe as a repair site for aircraft engines between 1940 and 1945. After U.S. forces occupied the area, it became a U.S. airfield on 14 November 1945, known as Field Y-73. Although Eschborn was the primary U.S. airfield for the Frankfurt area between 31 January 1947 and mid-1949, it soon proved to be too small to handle major operations. Over one million square feet of P.S.P. was moved from Eschborn to Rhein-Main, to provide 44 hardstands and many taxiways. A second runway was built in February and March 1949. Temporary housing was quickly erected there and at Army facilities in the Frankfurt area during the Berlin Airlift.

The housing problems were especially acute, and the nearby village of Zeppelinheim was confiscated to provide base housing. The inhabitants had to move, on one hour's notice. This village was not returned until 1955.

Open House

During the blockade, Rhein-Main A.B. hosted its first Open House on Air Force Day, 21 September 1948, to mark the first anniversary of the U.S. Air Force as a separate organization. Thousands of Germans came on 29 May 1949, to view the aircraft that were flying to Berlin. Military C-47, C-54, C-82, B-17 and a B-29 aircraft were open to the public, along with the new civilian Pan Am Boeing B-377 Stratocruiser. These were the first of many airshows the base would host, improving relationships among neighbors.

Wiesbaden

Wiesbaden was an important Luftwaffe fighter base during the war. When U.S. Forces captured the field, the Army gave it the name Y-80 until the Airlift when it was renamed Wiesbaden A.B. with Col. H.M. Wittkop as base commander. It played not only a major role airlifting food to Berlin, but 120,000 lb. of mail also arrived in Wiesbaden from Berlin.

The world-famous Kurhaus, located in downtown Wiesbaden, once a luxury hotel, was turned into the Eagles Club, operated by Special Services. It offered airmen a snack bar, ball room, concert hall, music rooms, language courses, and even a sports center. Many other elegant facilities were acquired by the military for their troops, such as the Opel swimming pool, and clay tennis courts.

The civilian terminal building at Rhein-Main in 1948. Lufthansa had not yet been given permission to operate; but other European airlines, notably B.E.A., SABENA, S.A.S., K.L.M., and Air France, as well as the American A.O.A., flew scheduled services into Frankfurt.

A C-54 comes in 'over the fence' at Rhein-Main. Note the newly-installed approach lights, making use of the recently-introduced P.S.P. (Pierced Steel Planking) for their construction.

This was one of the U.S. Air Force main hangars at Rhein-Main, easily able to accommodate the Douglas four-engined C-54s.

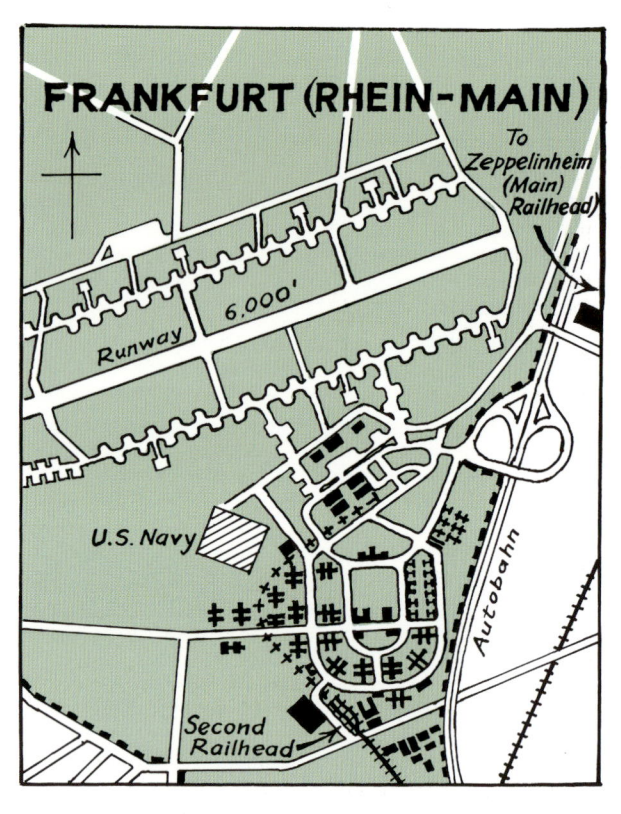

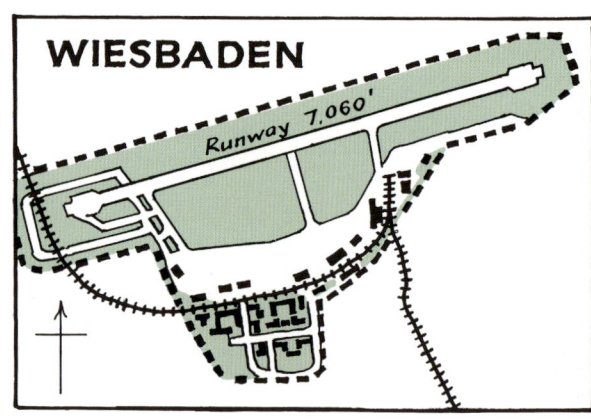

The Central Corridor Fields

Wunstorf
R.A.F. Wunstorf, located near Hanover, 150 miles west of Berlin, was originally a grass airfield and saw German night-fighter aircraft and light bombers between 1939 and 1940. The base was later used for pilot training. In 1946 the R.A.F. built a hard runway that was extended in concrete in 1947. At first an R.A.F. fighter base, it was rebuilt to handle 94 transport aircraft. Dakotas were hurriedly transferred there on 26–27 June 1948, and on 28 June, **Operation Knicker** began from Wunstorf providing the first supplies to Berlin, mainly for British troops.

Units at Wunstorf included: Nos. 40, 51, 99, 206 and 242 Squadrons: which operated a total of 39 Yorks, and three civilian air carriers; Skyways, B.S.A.A. and Airflight.

Fassberg
Completed by the Luftwaffe in 1936, Fassberg was one of its largest Air Bases. The construction cost, which included a nearby town for 2,500 people, totalled 750 million Reichs Marks. The local mayor, Hugo Weisner, was able to prevent the Luftwaffe from destroying the base before war's end. Until May 1947, the R.A.F. employed approximately 800 Germans. A concrete runway, 1,830 m (6,000 ft) long and 30 m (100 ft) wide, was completed during the Airlift.

The R.A.F. gave permission for the U.S.A.F. to use Fassberg. The British moved all their C-47s there on 19 July 1948, later transferring to Lübeck so that the U.S.A.F. could move three squadrons of C-54s to Fassberg. The 46 U.S.A.F. C-54s stationed at Fassberg began transporting coal on 21 August 1948.

Col. Dale D. Fisher was assigned as base commander. German employee numbers grew to 12,000. Quonset huts provided temporary housing at Camp Trauen for 5,000 single German civilian male employees. A rail line connected it to the base. Using 7,000 meters of old rail from the dismantled munitions factory at Unterlüss, this link was extended directly to the runway, simplifying the transport of coal, 200 to 300 trainwagons each day. Both Fassberg and Celle were vital for transporting coal and liquid fuel to Berlin, because of the shorter distance.

Fassberg became well known for Operation Santa Claus, in which military units in the States supplied thousands of packages with gifts for children in Berlin. The Commanding General of the French occupation troops, General Pierre König, donated the use of his private airplane, to assist in transporting packages collected in France.

540 Officers, 1,400 senior NCOs (Non-Commissioned Officers) and about 4,000 airmen were stationed at Fassberg. Aircraft from this base hauled 500,000 tons in 52,482 flights, with the final flight occurring on 27 August 1949.

Celle
The Luftwaffe had built Celle in 1935 as a training base. During the closing days of the war, Junkers Ju-88s of the Behelfs Beleuchter Staffel 1 (No. 1 Illuminator Squadron) were stationed there. The R.A.F. laid a P.S.P. runway, but when the U.S.A.F. arrived, a tarmac runway was built within three months for the total of 42 U.S.A.F. C-54s stationed there.

Formerly known as Wietzenbruch, Celle was a small, forgotten airfield before the Americans turned it into a major base of operations, because it was also near Fassberg. It was very practical for Airlift operations as it was on a major rail line to Hannover. The local population grew to more than 5,000 workers, working in 3 shifts, assisting in the handling operations. The Union Club was a favorite night spot. Almost 2,000 fräuleins found their way to Celle, to the dismay of the local community, who called it the Veronika-Invasion. A special concern was the rapid increase of venereal disease among soldiers. The military handled the housing situation for the 3,000 soldiers, by erecting temporary housing and by expropriating 264 local private homes.

The final flight from Celle to the U.S. occurred on 18 August 1949.

A U.S.A.F. C-54 approaches and touches down at Fassberg. (Photos courtesy Albert Lowe.)

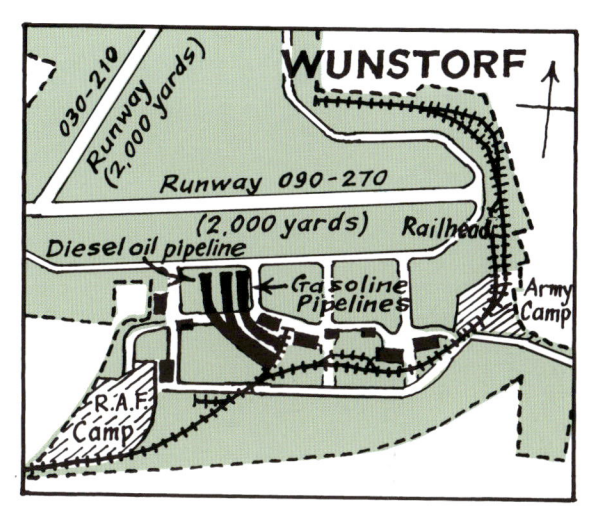

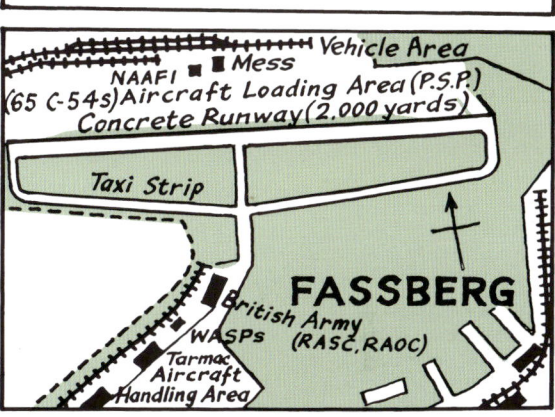

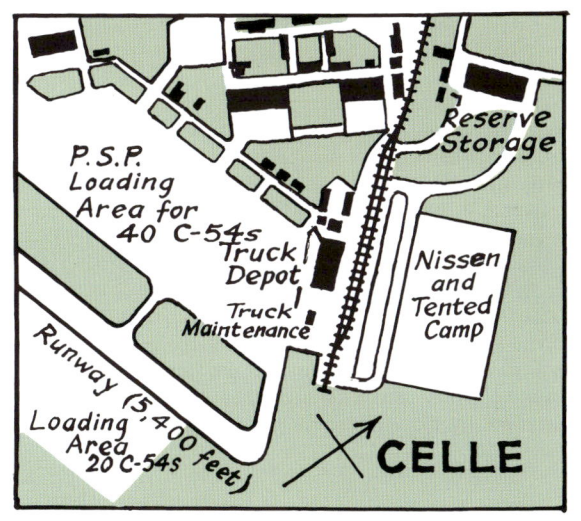

The Northern Corridor Fields

Hamburg

The civilian airport at Fuhlsbüttel, Hamburg, was the last airfield to be included in Berlin Airlift operations. It was first opened on 10 January 1911, as an airship base. After the World War of 1914–1918, it was used exclusively by heavier-than-air aircraft and in 1933 underwent a large expansion program. It suffered no damage from the Second World War and became a British R.A.F. base on 20 September 1945. Two P.S.P. runways were built shortly thereafter. In April 1948, construction of a concrete runway began, but was not completed until year's end. All civilian aircraft moved from Lübeck to Fuhlsbüttel on 5 October 1948. Flight Refuelling, along with Bond Air Services, Eagle Aviation, and World Air Freight, were the primary users and the Halton (Halifax bomber, converted as a freighter) was the aircraft used the most. In 1949, 12,433 Airlift flights originated from Fuhlsbüttel.

Lübeck

R.A.F. Station Lübeck was a former Luftwaffe base, built in 1935. Heinkel He-111 bombers and, in the closing days of the war, Junkers-Ju 88 fighters, operated from Lübeck. The R.A.F. began with Dakotas on 27 August 1948. A total of 108,000 sq.m. (more than a million square feet) of P.S.P. were laid, providing runways and hardstands. The R.A.F. flew 68,000 undernourished children or ill elderly civilians into Lübeck for treatment. The base was close to the Soviet Zone, only two miles away. The final aircraft bore the inscription:

"Positively the last load from Lübeck. Psalm 21, Verse 11: For they intended evil against thee: They imagined a mischievous device which they are not able to perform." It was a Dakota (KN 652) that departed on 23 September 1949.

The following units were stationed at Lübeck: No. 1 Dominion, R.A.A.F./ R.N.Z.A.F. Squadron; No. 2 Dominion, S.A.A.F. Squadron; R.A.F. 18, 46, and 53 Squadrons, operating a total of 42 Dakotas.

Schleswigland

This R.A.F. Station originally opened in 1935 as a civilian glider airfield, it was taken over by the Luftwaffe in 1938 and used thereafter as a night-fighter base. It had a concrete runway, for use by the Me-262 jet fighters that were deployed in the final months of the war.

During the Airlift, the runway was covered with 7 cm (3 in.) thick tarmac to withstand heavy use. More than 89,000

This picture clearly shows the extensive terminal building and the large hangar at Fühlsbuttel Airport at Hamburg. Two Avro Yorks and a Douglas C-47 Dakota are in the mid-distance, and another Dakota and a Lancastrian are on the concrete ramp. (Flughafen, Hamburg)

Like all the DC-3/C-47 variants, the Royal Air Force Dakota was a picture of elegant efficiency in the air.

sq.m. (about 950,000 sq. ft.) of P.S.P. were laid, to provide a large hardstand for parked aircraft. Schleswigland had underground fuel storage capable of holding 160,000 gallons. It had a practical loading area, which could handle 16 aircraft only a short distance from the rail yard with three train tracks.

R.A.F. 47 and 297 Squadrons maintained and operated 23 Hastings at Schleswigland. The first arrived on 1 November 1948, piloted by Sqdr. Leader P.J.S. Finlayson. Four civilian carriers, Lancashire Aircraft Corp., Westminster Airways, British American Air Services, and Scottish Airlines used the base, operating 11 Halton Tankers, which began to arrive 24 November 1948, with the remaining aircraft in January 1949.

On 6 September 1949, Flt. Lt. D.J. Harper flew the final Operation Plainfare mission from Schleswigland. R.A.F. Hastings from Schleswigland accounted for 49,981 tons.

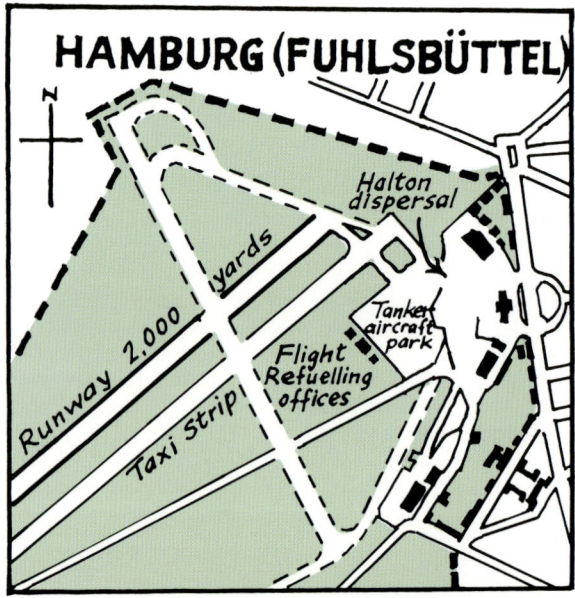

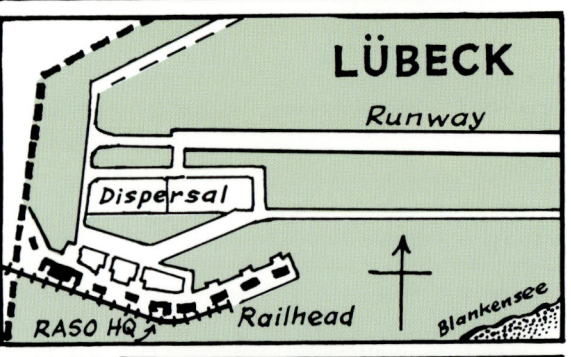

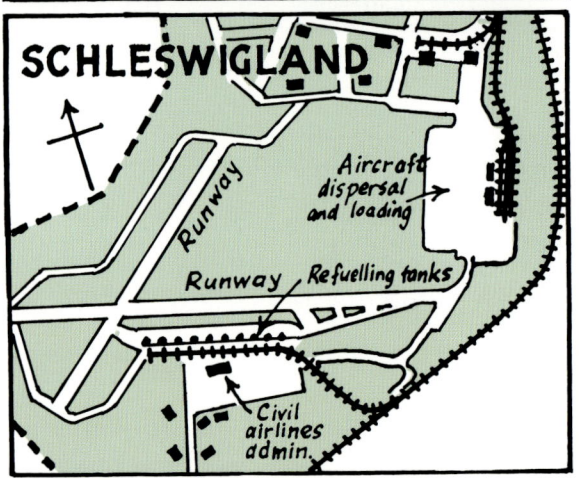

The Other Bases

The success or failure of the entire Airlift hinged upon the number of landings and takeoffs that could be made in Berlin. Tempelhof and Gatow soon proved to be too small to handle operations, so a third base at Tegel was built. Eight airfields (two U.S. and six R.A.F.) in western Germany were feeding supplies into three turnaround airfields in Berlin, to ensure the success of the Airlift in the long run. The U.S. Air Force also used the following bases, for spare parts supply and maintenance.

Erding
Erding Air Force Depot was a maintenance depot near Munich that provided wartime surplus spare parts, reconditioned spark plugs, balanced propellers, etc. common to C-47s and C-54s. The personnel processed, screened, and returned to active stock more than 30,000 tons of badly needed equipment, worth more than $126 million.

Oberpfaffenhofen
Oberpfaffenhofen was used for aircraft maintenance, beginning on 5 August 1948 until the operations were moved to Burtonwood, near Liverpool, England. The cold Bavarian winter would have hindered maintenance operations, even with improvised docks (see photograph).

R.A.F. Burtonwood
A huge wartime base, with a 70-mile perimeter, had been abandoned. A few old Lancaster bombers still remained on the airfield, with several hangars and control tower; and the four giant hangars, which could hold three C-54 aircraft each, were still usable.

The base reopened on 1 September 1948. C-54 aircraft were given a thorough cleaning in a large wash hangar. The accommodation and amenities at the field were not exactly the Ritz, but they improved, and eventually 2,000 U.S. personnel were stationed at Burtonwood. On 7 January 1949 a C-54 crashed north of the airfield, killing six, but this was the only fatal accident that occurred at the base.

Finkenwerder
This was an open stretch on the Elbe river, to the west of Hamburg. Royal Air Force Sunderlands and Aquila Airways Hythe flying boats departed from here to the Havel Lake, adjacent to Gatow airfield in Berlin. They were especially useful for carrying the essential supplies of salt, as their hulls were specially anodized to resist corrosion from salt water. Towards winter, when Havel Lake froze, they were replaced by Handley Page Halifax/Haltons, which were also specially anodized.

Improvisation: To overcome the harsh Central European winter, and in the absence of large hangars at Oberpfaffenhofen, engine removal for overhaul and other repairs were aided by improvised docks. One is seen here in the course of hasty construction. (Smithsonian Institution)

A Royal Air Force Sunderland flying boat at Havel Lake. Conveniently, the loads, mainly of salt, could be transferred directly to barges, which were towed into the center of Berlin. (H.M.S.O.)

Maintenance

Formidable Timetable
Good maintenance was one of General Tunner's most important objectives, and 64% of all aircraft were always ready to fly. Propeller aircraft required a great deal of maintenance, caused by the vibrating engines and short life span of parts. 6% of all aircraft were grounded because of work in the shops; 10% through scheduled maintenance; 9% through major maintenance work which was done in Oberpfaffenhofen or Burtonwood, England; while another 11% were grounded because of unscheduled maintenance work.

Aircraft required on-line maintenance after every 25 hours of flight. After 200 hours, a major inspection was performed at **Oberpfaffenhofen,** near Munich, known to the airmen as Oberhuffin' Puffin', which had opened on 5 August 1948. Aircraft were washed with kerosene and water on open-air ramps. Later these inspections shifted to **Burtonwood,** because of anticipated harsh Bavarian winters. But Burtonwood could not handle the large volume, so responsibility returned to the local squadrons, working 12-hour work days, every day. The situation improved shortly after Christmas 1948, when Secretary of the Air Force, Stuart Symington, visited Airlift bases. Personnel and spare parts were rapidly forthcoming and emergency housing ordered.

Trans-Atlantic Supply Chain
Rhein-Main became the central warehouse and distribution center for spare parts for C-54s, while **Erding** provided supplies common to all aircraft. At 11:00 a.m. each morning, a list of required parts was cabled to Air Force Supply Headquarters at Wright Field (later Wright-Patterson Air Force Base) in Dayton, Ohio. These lists covered 20 pages with 20 items each. In Ohio, these items were designated Vittles and given top priority. In emergencies, items were ordered from the U.S. Supply Depot in Middletown, Pennsylvania, without bureaucratic procedures. All supplies were flown to Germany from Westover AFB at Chicopee Falls, Massachusetts, either by military aircraft or civilian air carriers. Those C-54s returning to Germany, after their 1,000-hour maintenance in the United States, were also loaded with these supplies. Once parts and supplies could be stockpiled, only emergency parts were airlifted to Germany. The Airlift soon caused a shortage of spare parts in the United States, and even in the Pacific theater, so that sizable replacement parts orders to the manufacturers had to be made.

Supplementary Help (U.S.A.)
After 1,000 hours flight time, every aircraft received a comprehensive overhaul in the United States, either at **Texas Engineering & Mfg. Co.(TEMCO)** in Dallas; **Aircraft Engineering & Maintenance Co. (AEMCO)** (a division of **Trans-Ocean Airlines Inc.**) in Oakland; or **Lockheed Aircraft Service Corp.** in Sayville, Long Island. The Navy routed its R5D to VR-44 Squadron stationed at Moffett Naval Air Station near San Francisco, while occasionally sending aircraft to Lockheed Aircraft Service Corp. at Burbank. Approximately 3,000 people were overhauling Airlift aircraft, with 25 each month at TEMCO alone. The Pratt & Whitney R-2000-9 and R-2000-11 engines for C-54s were overhauled at Kelly A.F.B., San Antonio, Texas, flown to Westover A.F.B., then on to Germany.

The number of aircraft actually deployed reached a maximum of 354 aircraft, often with more than 100 aircraft in the maintenance system. Usually about 240 aircraft were in service in Germany at any given time.

Supplementary Help (Germany)
Good mechanics were in short supply. Anti-fraternization laws prevented the military from hiring well-qualified former Luftwaffe mechanics to assist in aircraft maintenance. Tunner quickly had this law changed. Former Luftwaffe Major General Hans Detlev von Rohden was asked to assist the U.S.A.F.E. in locating mechanics. He spoke English and helped to translate the maintenance manuals into German. Bilingual American mechanics were assigned as supervisors until the Germans were familiar with the C-54. Soon the German mechanics outnumbered Americans. The fear of Germans sabotaging the Airlift was forgotten and mechanics of both nations were soon working together successfully. Twenty-seven incidents occurred that were believed to be sabotage; only 4 were proven.

Maintenance Problems
The U.S.A.F.E. stripped the C-54s of unnecessary safety equipment and other items, thereby providing more payload. Tests conducted at Burtonwood showed that 2,500 lb. could be saved on each airplane. The short flights and frequent heavy landings and take-offs on poorly prepared runways placed extreme wear on engines, landing gears, tires and brakes. Good maintenance was vital and coal dust which managed to enter almost every piece of equipment did not help.

Spare parts quickly became a problem. A mass of supplies and spare parts, left over from the Second World War was stored in the huge depot in Erding, near Munich, but no records existed and no one knew what was available, how much and where. A supply of windshield wipers, estimated to last six months, was used up in two weeks. 60,000 spark plugs had to be reconditioned each month. The shortage of spare engines led to the use of older engines which had been in storage in the U.S., but which had less horsepower. An aircraft fitted with two different types of engines was difficult for a pilot to handle.

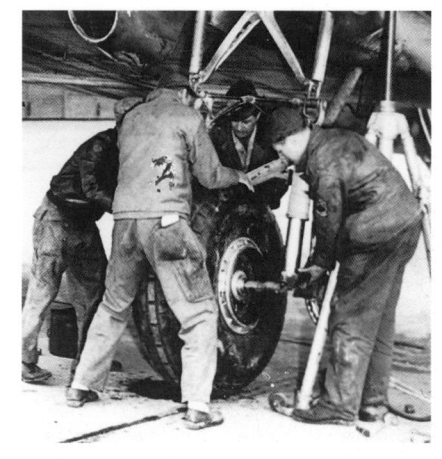

Open-air maintenance was standard procedure in Germany during the Airlift. A C-54 engine is inspected (left) while a C-47 landing gear receives a new wheel (right). (U.S.A.F.)

"90% of Aviation is on the Ground"

Checking the plugs on a C-47. 9(U.S.A.F.)

General Tunner took a special interest in the maintenance of the Airlift aircraft. "90% of aviation is on the ground," as Clement Keys said back in 1929. Tunner is seen here discussing local problems at Oberpfaffenhofn. (Smithsonian Institution)

Occasionally, C-47s could be maintained under cover, in a hangar; but the C-54s were too big for the installations readily available, and required special docking in the open air (see page 39). (U.S.A.F.)

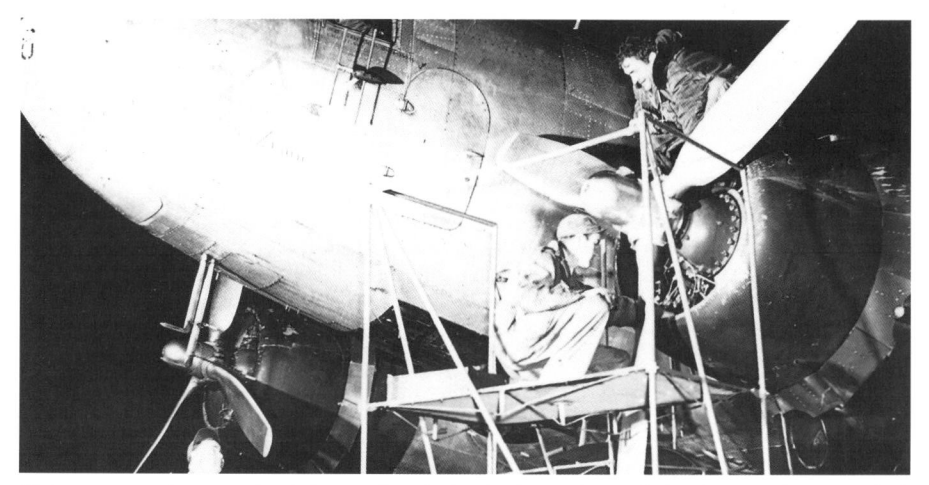

Maintenance work went on by night as well as during the day, under arc-lights. Even so, there were dark spots, and awkward spots, requiring a little ingenuity and contortion to reach. (U.S.A.F.)

41

Airfield Construction

Inadequate Fields

When the Berlin Airlift began, most airfields were inadequate for heavy transport aircraft such as the C-54. The Luftwaffe had never deployed a heavy bomber force, and therefore did not need paved runways. Now, in 1948, a concerted effort began as the western Allies stepped into the breach.

Foundations for another runway at Tempelhof are laid down, mostly by using rubble from Berlin's bombed buildings. The two pictures below illustrate the international aspects of cooperation. The airfield is at Tegel, in the French zone; the workforce was German. (U.S.A.F.)

Here, at the R.A.F. base at Celle, a substantial runway, with a bearing strength able to cope with four-engined C-54 heavy transports, is rapidly constructed. A dozen steamrollers are at work—although they seem to have abandoned any attempt at echelon formation. A special branch from the railroad (right) brought materials. The whole operation was conducted as in a wartime emergency. (H.M.S.O.)

42

P.S.P., or the Marston Mat

The Marston Mat

During the course of the War, the Germans had never developed paved runways for their aircraft. The heavy American aircraft could not land on grass fields unless they were perfectly dry—seldom the case for very long in Europe. During the early period of the Berlin Airlift this problem had to be solved quickly. The answer was found in the Marston Mat, designed by **Gerald G. Greulich** of the **Carnegie Illinois Steel Co.** In November 1941, the Chief of the Army Air Forces, Gen. H.H. 'Hap' Arnold, visited a small maneuver ground, along U.S. Route 1, near Marston, N.C., where steel planks, 10 ft. long and 15 inches wide, had been interlocked to create a temporary runway. The mats weighed 62.5 lb. each and within only a few weeks, 60,000 of them had formed a 5,000 foot long and 150 foot wide runway. During World War II, these became known as **Marston Mats** and many military airfields were equipped with them (often within days). One or two men could lift a single section easily and repairs could be carried out quickly. Marston Mat runways could withstand landing operations of aircraft with a total weight of 60,000 lb.. During the war, the weight of aircraft increased from the 55,000 lb. of a B-17 Flying Fortress or B-24 Liberator to the 125,000 lb. of a B-29 Superfortress. These larger aircraft required paved runways.

P.S.P.

After the War, the name was changed to **P.S.P. (Pierced Steel Planking)**. They formed many of the essential runways and most of the paved ramp space, hardstands, roads, sidewalks and even landing approach light towers used during the Berlin Airlift.

The constant pounding of heavy aircraft landing caused much damage to the P.S.P. runways at Tempelhof and a work force of 225 were needed to keep the runways in useable condition. Nevertheless, this remarkably simple and unspectacular invention assisted greatly in the success of the Berlin Airlift.

Rather like using giant-sized Erector or Meccano sets, the P.S.P. could be used for other improvised purposes. Here it is being adapted to provide a tower for a high-powered light beacon.

A Royal Army Service Corps sergeant major observes the finer points of laying down P.S.P. at Gatow. The workers were hastily recruited from Berlin's unemployed and volunteer workers. (H.M.S.O.)

The Gatow runway is almost finished, with acres of P.S.P. laid with precision. The strips have been delivered in a Fairchild C-82, whose rear access door was ideal for the purpose. (U.S.A.F.)

U.S. Scheduled Airline Help

DC-4

'American Overseas Airlines' fuselage titles were later amended to read 'American Airlines System.'

Payload 19,500 lb. ■ **Speed 170 mph** ■ **Pratt & Whitney R-2000 (1,450 hp) x 4** ■ **Max. Gross Take-off Weight 68,000 lb.** ■ **Range 1,000 st. miles**
Note: Max. Gross Take-off Weights varied, from 62,000 to 73,800 lb. (see also page 23).

A Call to Arms

Such was the suddenness of the Soviet blockade that the U.S. armed forces were not immediately prepared to meet the logistical demand, as their transport aircraft had been relatively inactive after the demands of the Second World War came to an end. They were under 'care and maintenance only' at various bases. At first, even a couple of aged **Boeing B-17 Flying Fortresses** were drafted into action again, carrying ten tons of food at the early stages of the Airlift. They had tried to drop coal but only succeeded in spreading pulverized coal, as it disintegrated on hitting the ground.

Fortunately, a call to arms from the commercial airlines brought a quick and energetic response. One scheduled airline was on the spot already, and some of the non-scheduled irregular carriers, who were skilled at charter work, proud to be able to demonstrate their capability and to aid the effort, came to the rescue.

American Overseas Airlines (A.O.A.)

The international division of American Airlines was created by the purchase of American Export Airlines on 5 December 1945. Responsible for service to all the countries of northern Europe, including points in the U.K., Germany, and Scandinavia, it had made 15,000 Atlantic crossings by September 1947.

On 2 March 1948, it was authorized to start an **Internal German Service (I.G.S.)** from Frankfurt to Berlin, using the ubiquitous DC-4, the civilian variant of the military C-54.

When the Blockade began, A.O.A. entered the fray immediately, on 26 June 1948. Six DC-4s and a London-based DC-3 (C-47) were pressed into service, and, as the accompanying photograph shows, the airline made more than a token contribution to the Airlift effort.

Pan American and T.W.A.

Pan American Airways made only five flights to Berlin during the Airlift. One of these was a DC-3/C-47, in which Capt. George Price entered into the spirit of the humanitarian emergency. Pan Am was not authorized to serve Berlin, and George was severely reprimanded on his return to Frankfurt. **Transcontinental & Western Air (T.W.A.)**, later to become TransWorld Airlines, also made seven Airlift flights across the Atlantic.

There were often excuses to celebrate achievements in load-carrying records. (John Provan)

44

U.S. Non-scheduled Airline Help

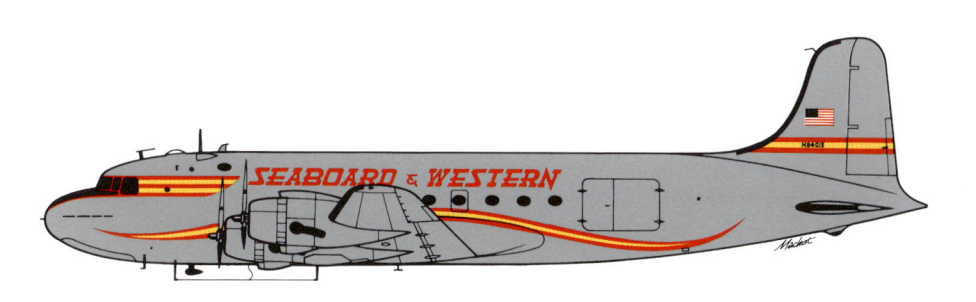

Specialized Freighter
At the end of the War, scores of entrepreneur aviators started up their own small airlines, equipped with their own flying knowledge and with some bargain-basement war-surplus aircraft, mostly C-47s and C-54s. One of these was **Seaboard & Western Airlines,** organized on 16 September 1946, and starting trans-Atlantic charter flights from New York to Europe on 10 May 1947—a year before the Berlin Airlift began. It had a few C-54s and its European base was Luxemburg, the diminutive country that was the refuge of the non-scheduled operators. It was conveniently located near Frankfurt, and Seaboard made 106 flights in support of Operation Vittles.

The Ubiquitous Orvis
Another prominent non-scheduled airline of the post-war period was **Transocean Air Lines,** founded on 1 June 1946 by a group of ex-United Air Lines crew members, led by **Orvis Nelson.** Of all the international charter and non-scheduled airlines, this was possibly the greatest of them all, and its slogan was "we fly anything, anywhere." This included several series of flights for emigrants and refugees, itinerant fishermen, or pilgrims to Mecca. Equipped with C-54s, and armed with crews who were prepared to take on any challenge, Transocean could take the Berlin Airlift in its stride, and made 50 Airlift flights. Even more, its maintenance base at Oakland, California, was one of the finest in the world, and was prominent in restoring decommissioned C-54s back into working order. One of these, 'Workhorse Harry,' made 1,943 Airlift flights, carrying coal. Another C-54, sent to Oakland for recuperation, yielded 243 lb. of coal dust. Orvis had it packed in jars and given to his employees to stimulate productivity.

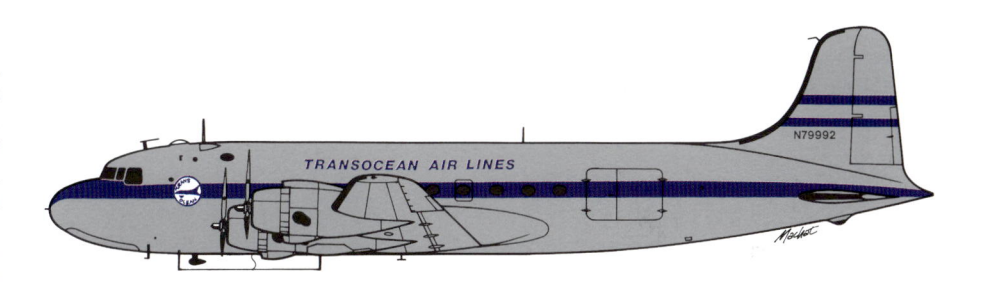

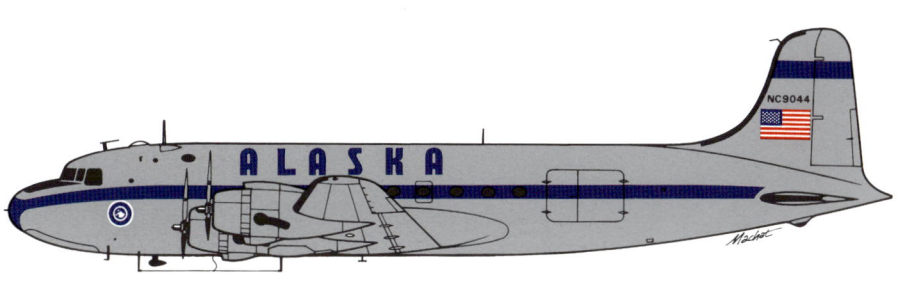

Another airline that supplemented the Irregular Carriers (as the Civil Aeronautics Board called that happy band of extrovert flying adventurers) was, rather surprisingly, one from far-off Alaska. Under the aggressive leadership of **James Wooten,** one of the local operators (classified later as a Territorial) was enterprisingly seeking other fields of activity beyond its local horizons. **Alaska Airlines** flew 87 trips from New York to Germany. It also brought eleven loads of German War brides back to America late in 1948.

The Survivor
Curiously, of all the many commercial operators, scheduled and non-scheduled, American and British, who participated in the Airlift, Alaska Airlines is the only one that continues to operate under the same name today.

The rather austere markings of this era were derived from the MATS military-style colors, and preceded the more decorative color schemes created by America's most noted industrial designers in the early-1950s.

45

Tunner's "Jungle Drums"

Reinforcements
A shortage of personnel as the Airlift began was a problem. Pilots were averaging seven hours sleep every 36 hours. Sergeant Donald Fromme recalls asking his roommate: "Hey, are we getting up or going to bed?" A pilot was not allowed to fly more than 110 hours per month but because each airplane had to be kept flying 270 per hours month, each aircraft required three crews. A replacement training unit was established at Great Falls Air Force Base in Montana, to provide replacement pilots. By December 1948, sufficient replacements were available and could then be rotated after six months duty. Although 1,258 pilots were flying by July 1949, the estimated requirement of 1,322 had still not been reached.

Another problem was that the Air Force's Air Transport Command (A.T.C.) and the Naval Air Transport Service (NATS) duplicated each other on many routes. A.T.C. had 22,000 personnel and 366 aircraft and NATS had 6,300 personnel with 84 aircraft, too small to sustain a massive long-term airlift. Not until 3 May 1948, did Defense Secretary Forrestal create the **Military Air Transport Service (MATS)** as the single organization. It began operating on 1 June 1948. 2,800 NATS personnel along with some aircraft were transferred to the Air Force's MATS on 1 July 1948. This rapid changeover was needed, as the Berlin Airlift had begun before total restructuring of the services had been completed.

Instrument Flying
General Tunner made instrument flying mandatory, regardless of weather conditions and time of day. Also he did not allow pilots to make a second attempt at landing in Berlin. If a pilot missed his landing, for whatever reason, he would return to his home base. This prevented confusion and needless backup of aircraft in holding patterns.

The Rhythm
The Airlift had a certain rhythm which guaranteed success. Each aircraft was assigned a fixed hardstand position at its assigned base. When an aircraft touched down, it had 4 minutes to reach its position. After it was parked, the refuelling, small maintenance work, and loading occurred simultaneously. Manifests were prepared, giving detailed listings of the commodities, for proper loading, which took 1 hour. Engines started, it would take 4 minutes more to taxi to the runway, another 2 minutes for clearance and takeoff. The flight from Rhein-Main to Tempelhof took 1 hr 45 min.; and from Wiesbaden 1 hr 50 min.

Aircraft from Rhein-Main and Wiesbaden, transporting food to Berlin, would fly towards Fulda before entering the corridor. The pilot would then radio, "This is Baker Easy one-fourteen departing Fulda." All east-bound aircraft heading to Berlin were called 'Baker Easys' while all aircraft returning were called 'Baker Willies.' The numbers were the hardstand position numbers. Aircraft flew the corridor at three different levels, 4,000, 6,000, and 8,000 feet, each two minutes apart. Once an airplane reached Berlin, the Ground Control would radio, "Baker Easy one-fourteen, we have you at 1,000 feet" and guide the plane down.

The scheduling, the loading, flight operations, landing, and unloading were perfectly timed so that the maximum usage of the available airplanes and ground facilities was ensured. By Easter 1949, the initial rate of one aircraft movement every three minutes was rapidly increased to one movement every minute. This rhythm was like jungle drums and would become General Tunner's trademark.

Rapid Turnaround
Once landed at Tempelhof, aircraft took 5 minutes to reach the hardstand and shut down all engines. Vehicles were dispatched to each aircraft, wooden ramps assisted in unloading, and fork-lifts were used when needed. One jeep would come by, providing weather information and clearance. A second jeep operated as a mobile snack bar. General Tunner was very keen about having two beautiful Berliners work at these snack bars, "so that the men would have something to look at." Although the food was good, pilots nicknamed these mobile snack bars, the 'roach coach.' While the pilots and crew were being taken care of, the aircraft were unloaded, generally requiring 35 minutes each. Some were also reloaded in Berlin, with manufactured products, empty coal sacks, mail, or other provisions. These deliveries of manufactured goods were important for Berlin's economy, as it kept industries in production and created employment. An average of 350 tons were flown out every day.

Several soldiers would start engines with the help of a jeep equipped with a gasoline-powered electric generator. The aircraft would taxi out to the runway, taking 3 minutes. Clearance given, it would be in the air 4 minutes later. The average turnaround time for aircraft from an unloading base (Berlin) was a remarkable 49 minutes. All the more amazing, considering that the runways were made of P.S.P. Tunner wrote: "A force of a couple of hundred men equipped with new landing mats, sand, and asphalt, lined the runways. As soon as a plane roared by, they'd jump out and make what repairs they could, jump back out of the way when the next plane came by."

"Like a Damn Coal Mine"
Aircraft from Fassberg landed at Tegel, while aircraft from Celle landed at Gatow. These bases handled primarily the transport of coal. An airman told the story: "We had 50 lb. bags of coal stacked two high and four across, and even with the cargo door removed, that infernal black dust made its way in and on everything, including your eyes, hair, nose and lungs. It was like being in a damn coal mine! And minus that cargo door, it got pretty cold during the winter months

This line-up of nine C-54s at Rhein-Main illustrates the intensity of the high-frequency Airlift operations. (Gloria Wenk)

Marching to Different Drums

Radar Approaches
Radar-assisted approaches were a new development. Jack Bennett, from A.O.A., recalled: "The radar coverage from the ground was incredibly accurate. If our airplane crept up or fell back, even a few feet, on the aircraft preceding us, radar would warn us to adjust our airspeed by a minuscule knot. We couldn't believe it was possible to fly this accurately. Viewed from the radar screen on the ground, the aircraft appeared as individual green pearls, as perfectly spaced as on a woman's necklace, all moving with metronome regularity to Berlin." The radar-assisted approaches were new for many pilots and invaluable for the often foggy weather, poor visibility, and the difficult final approach into Tempelhof.

By 18 August 1948, the air corridors to Berlin were equipped with flight aids to ensure safe winter airlift operations. The U.S. Air Force's Airways and Air Communication Services was responsible for radio navigation aids, control towers, radio beacons, radio equipment, and air traffic control facilities. Procedures developed during the Airlift played a major role in the development of modern air traffic systems, as we know them today and would also apply to the Korean War, a short time later.

Pros and Cons
While the 'jungle drum' system worked well, there were some disadvantages, as there were limits to the number of aircraft that could be accommodated at one time on an airfield. A block system used a four-hour period for despatching, later reduced to one hour, and this reduced the time wasted on the ground, with aircraft ready to depart, with engines idling. Later, the flow was organized for all flights to converge at a fixed radio beacon, and the efficiency of arrivals, loading and unloading, and departures, measurably improved.

Royal Air Force Procedures
Royal Air Force aircraft were fitted with radar navigational equipment, including Distance Measuring Equipment (D.M.E.) and all R.A.F. crews included a navigator. They were therefore able to arrive at a given point at a given time, with a reasonable degree of accuracy, irrespective of the speed and altitude. U.S. aircraft did not carry navigators, and relied largely on radio compasses. They therefore had to calculate their ground speed, based on forecast winds, the accuracy of which was variable.

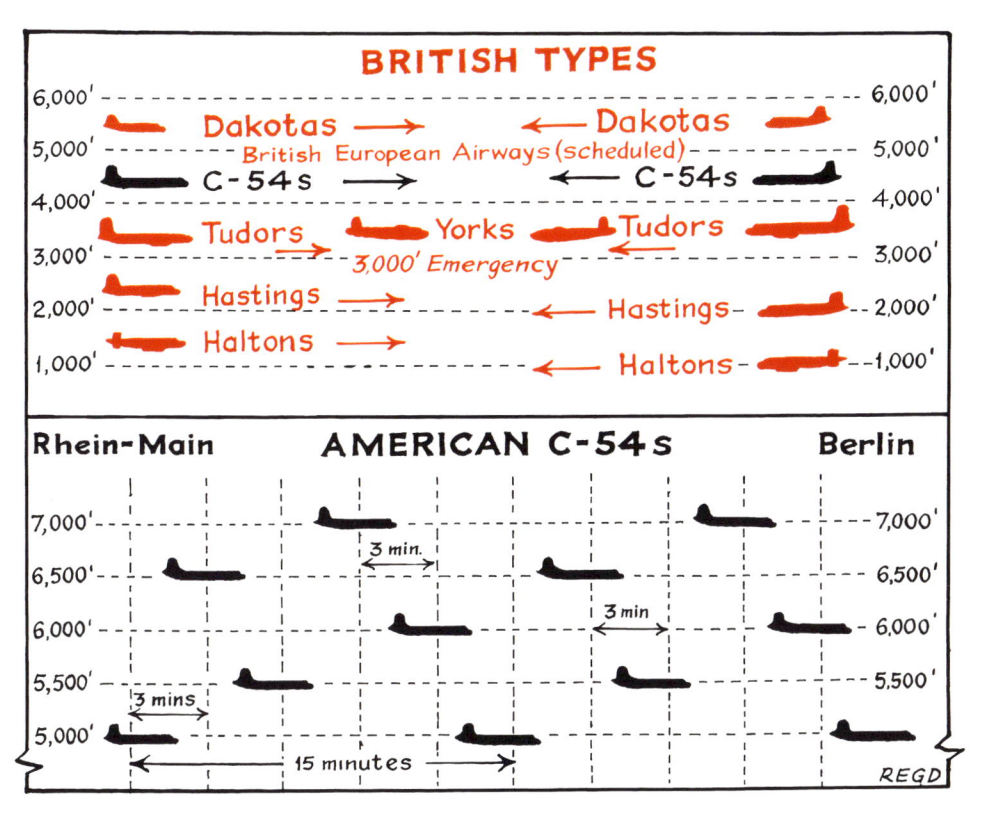

In contrast to the U.S. procedures, in which the aircraft fleet was of one type (the C-54), and therefore all of the same speed, the British deployed a variety of different types, of varying speeds. This demanded careful operational control, allocating different altitudes to the individual aircraft.

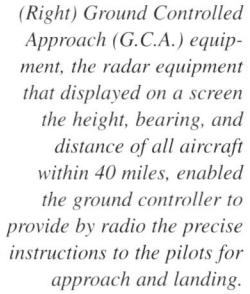

(Right) Ground Controlled Approach (G.C.A.) equipment, the radar equipment that displayed on a screen the height, bearing, and distance of all aircraft within 40 miles, enabled the ground controller to provide by radio the precise instructions to the pilots for approach and landing.

Bombers to Freighters

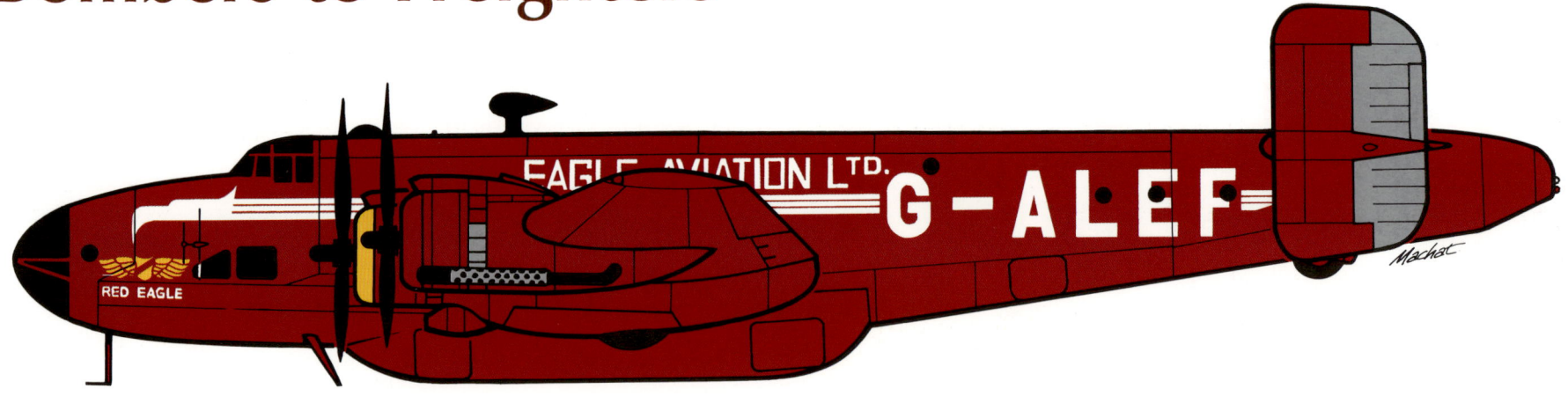

Harold Bamberg's Halifax *Red Eagle*

Payload 15,500 lb. ■ Speed 185 mph ■ Bristol Hercules 100 (1,650 hp) x 4 ■ Max. Gross Take-off Weight 68,000 lb. ■ Range 1,800 st. miles ■ Span 104 feet ■ Length 74 feet ■ Height 22 feet

Bomber Force

About 40% of all R.A.F. bombers of the Second World War were Halifaxes. During the Berlin Airlift they were used mainly as freighters, with extra capacity added in a detachable pannier fitted underneath the fuselage. The Halifax was used for general freight or as a tanker, and, when Lake Havel froze over, to carry salt, replacing the Sunderland flying boats. 8,000 lb of salt could be carried in the pannier, which was separated from the aircraft controls, thus protecting them from corrosion. An Eagle Halifax, G-AIAP, made the last civilian sortie into Berlin on 15 August 1949.

Harold Bamberg's Halifax C.VIII Red Eagle *made a colorful contrast with the usually drab metal aircraft fleets used on the Airlift. (Harold Bamberg)*

This picture of the Red Eagle *illustrates the versaitility of the Halifax in adapting the bomb bay for cargo. (Jackson Collection)*

Lancashire Aircraft Corporation Haltons carried more than 15,000 tons of liquid fuel into Berlin during the Airlift. (Jackson Collection)

Halifax of British American Air Services (B.A.A.S.), a London-based charter company. (Jackson Collection)

Halifax Mark C.VIII of Westminster Airways, whose aircraft carried both general cargo and liquid fuel. (Jackson Collection)

Handley Page Halifax/Halton

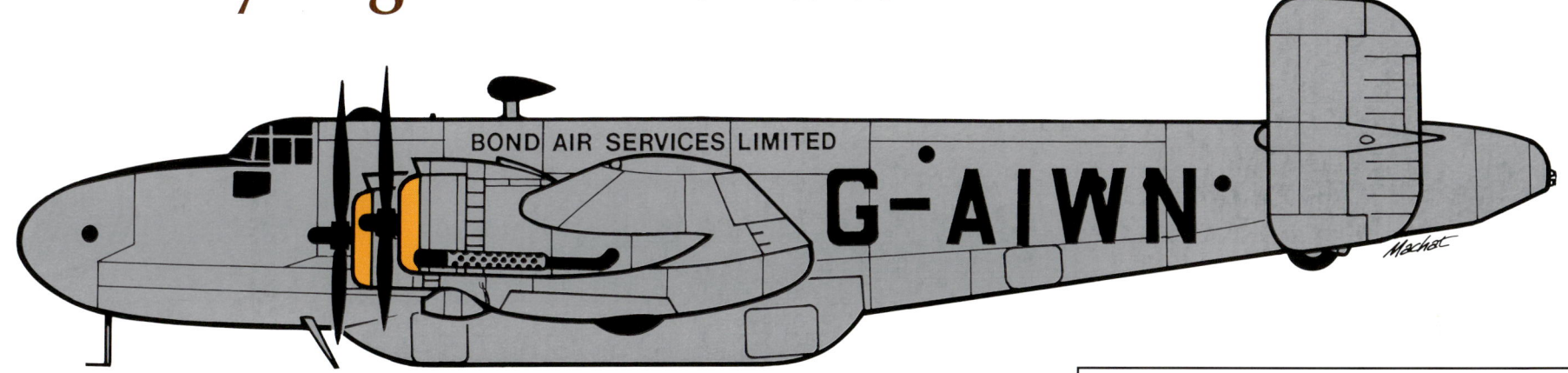

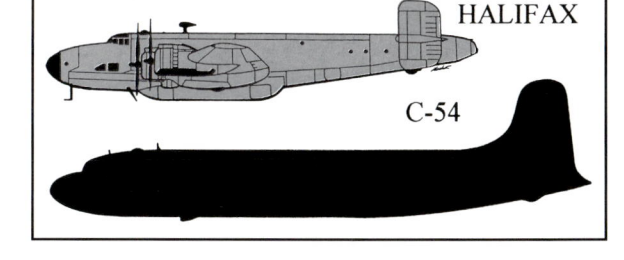

Halton Conversion

Strictly, the name Halton applied only to those Halifaxes that were converted to passenger airliners by B.O.A.C., which, in the immediate post-war years, was desperately in need of aircraft, and was limited in its dollar funds to buy American transports. The enterprising Freddie Laker, who established Aviation Traders as an aircraft engineering company at Southend, Essex, supplied Bond Air Services with its entire fleet of Halifax freighters.

One of World Air Freight's three Halifaxes. (Jackson Collection)

One of Bond Air Services' Halifaxes, in its austere minimum markings. This was a Mark C.IX. (Jackson Collection)

The metallic nose and the larger windows on this Bond Air Services aircraft reveal its previous brief life as a B.O.A.C. Halton. (Jackson Collection)

The Halifax/Halton Fleet Record (8,162 sorties, 52,811 tons)

Airline	Aircraft Registrations	Freighter Sorties	Freighter Tonnage	Tanker Sorties	Tanker Tonnage
British American Air Services	G-AIAR, G-AKBB, G-AKGN	97	525	564	3938
Bond Air Services	G-AHDN, G-AHDO, G-AHDP, G-AHDS, G-AHDT, G-AHDU, G-AHDW, G-AHDX, G-AIOI, G-AIWN, G-ALON, G-ALOS	2,577	17,131	—	—
Eagle Aviation	G-AIAP, G-AIAR, G-ALEF, G-AJBL	1,054	7,304	—	—
Lancashire Aircraft Corporation	G-AHCX, G-AHWN, G-AHYH, G-AIHV, G-AIHY, G-AILO, G-AJZY, G-AJZZ, G-AKBJ, G-AKBK, G-AKEC, G-AKXT, G-ALBZ	183	1,215	2,577	15,198
Skyflight	G-AIWP, G-AKBR	40	276	—	—
World Air Freight	G-AKAC, G-AKGZ, G-AKTC	526	3,703	—	—
Westminster Airways	G-AHDL, G-AHDM, G-AHDV, G-AHNW	176	928	368	2,592
TOTAL	(41 aircraft)	4,653	31,083	3,509	21,728

Avro Workhorses — Tudors...

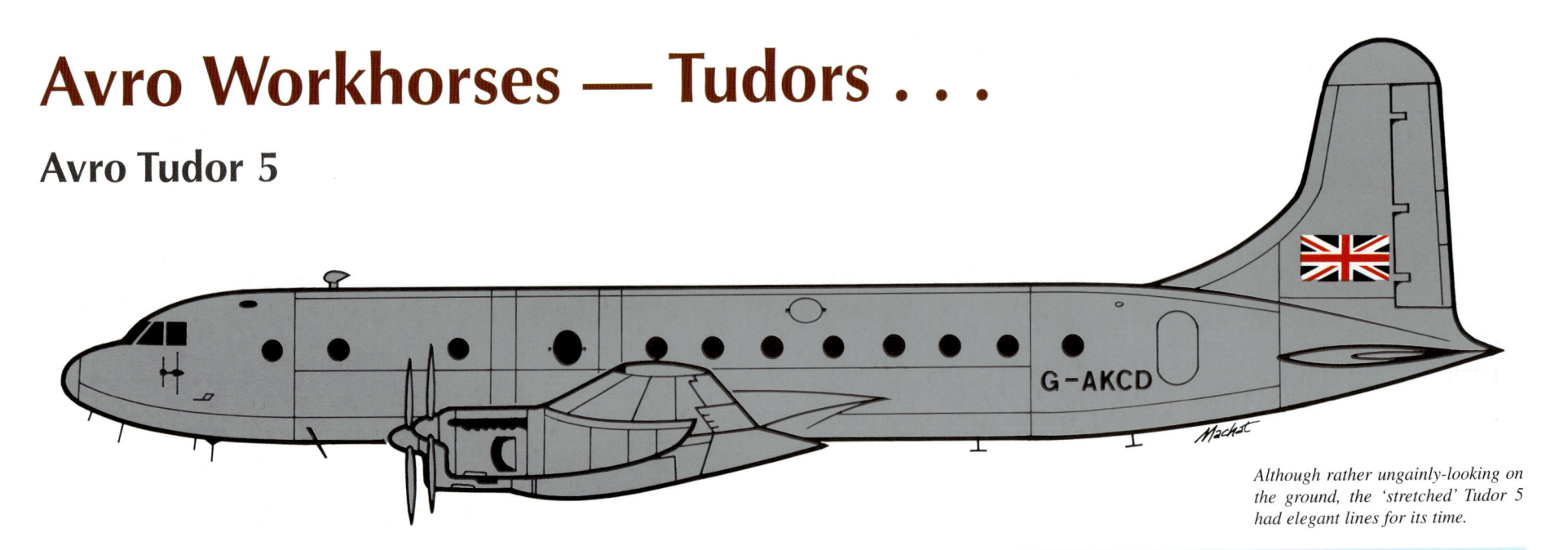

Avro Tudor 5

Although rather ungainly-looking on the ground, the 'stretched' Tudor 5 had elegant lines for its time.

Payload 17,950 lb. ■ Speed 185 mph ■ Rolls-Royce Merlin 623 (1,760 hp) x 4 ■ Max. Gross Take-off Weight 80,000 lb. ■ Range 1,500 st. miles ■ Span 120 feet ■ Length 106 feet ■ Height 24 feet

The Avro 688 Tudor

This Merlin-engined type was not a successful airliner, but it was often in the headlines during the early postwar years, mainly because of several accidents, including two disappearances over the Atlantic. But the Mark 5 version was a good load-carrier, and performed sterling service on the Airlift. B.S.A.A. pilot Peter Duffey declared it to climb better than the Argonaut (B.O.A.C.'s Canadian Merlin-engined DC-4) but was susceptible to ground-looping. Carrying 2,000 gallons of DERV (diesel fuel) in large tanks, the pilots had to climb in through the roof hatch. The pilots brought home cuckoo-clocks as souvenirs, craft-made near Wunstorf.

Some Tudors used on the Airlift were Mark Is, such as G-AGRH of B.S.A.A. (Jackson Collection)

An Airflight Tudor 2 of Airflight prepares to take off at Gatow, loaded with liquid fuel. (Gloria Wenk)

... and Yorks

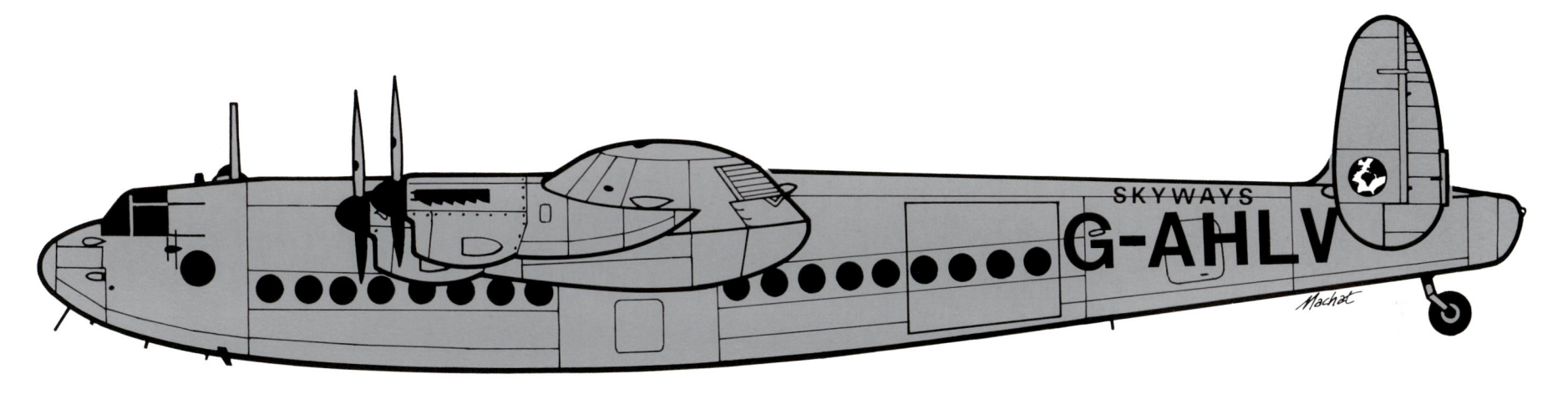

Payload 20,500 lb. ■ **Speed 185 mph** ■ **Rolls-Royce Merlin 502 (1,620 hp) x 4** ■ **Max. Gross Take-off Weight 70,000 lb.** ■ **Range 1,000 st. miles** ■ **Span 102 feet** ■ **Length 79 feet** ■ **Height 17 feet**

The Avro 685 York

Developed from the Lancaster bomber, this Merlin-powered transport was a good load-carrier. First introduced by the R.A.F. in 1942, 253 were built, and went into post-war commercial service with B.O.A.C., B.S.A.A., two British state airline corporations; and FAMA, in Argentina. It was the backbone of the Royal Air Force Airlift, carrying 61% of the load and accounting for 42% of the total R.A.F. aircraft movements. During the Airlift, the British charter operator, Skyways, also operated Yorks.

The British Civilian Tudor/York Fleet Record

Airline	Aircraft Registrations	Freighter Sorties	Freighter Tonnage	Tanker Sorties	Tanker Tonnage
Airflight	G-AGRY, G-AKBY	85	749	836	7,235
British South American Airways	G-AGBZ, G-AGRH, G-AGRJ, G-AKCA, G-AKCB, G-AKCC, G-AKCD	231	2,312	2,331	19,813
TOTAL	(9 Tudors)	316	3,061	3,167	27,047
Skyways	G-ALBX, G-AHFI, G-AHLV	1,081	10,175	13	109
TOTAL	(3 Yorks)	1,081	10,175	13	109

Three Avro Yorks at Wunstorf. These aircraft comprised almost two thirds of the R.A.F.'s contribution to the Berlin Airlift. (John Provan)

An R.A.F. Avro York had the honour of carrying the 1,000,000th ton of supplies into Berlin. (John Provan)

The Air Tankers — Lancasters, Lincolns, . . .

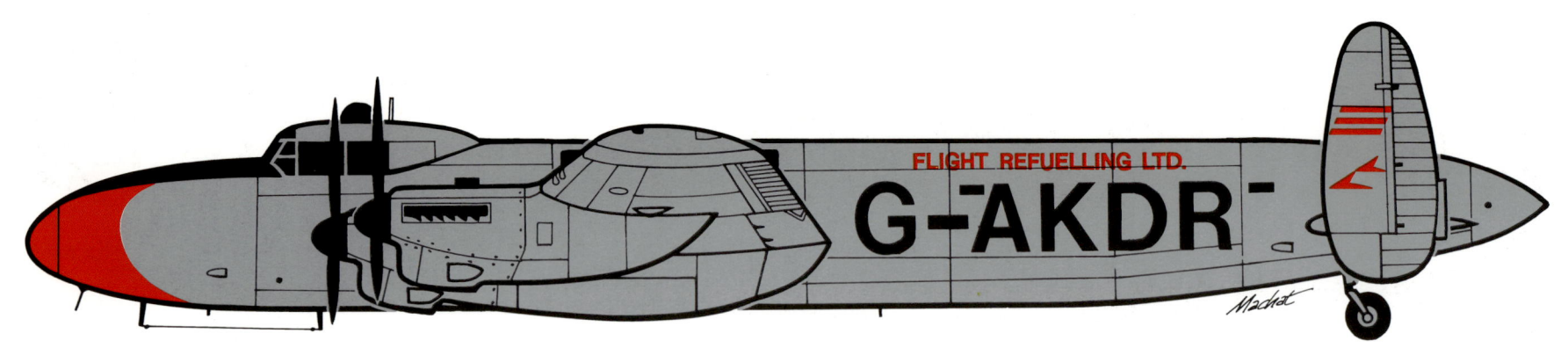

Lancaster of Flight Refuelling Ltd.

Payload 18,600 lb. ■ **Speed 185 mph** ■ **Rolls-Royce Merlin 85 (1,750 hp) x 4** ■ **Max. Gross Take-off Weight 65,000 lb.** ■ **Range 1,000 st. miles** ■ **Span 102 feet** ■ **Length 77 feet** ■ **Height 20 feet**

When the call came for all aid to the Berlin Airlift, the British charter companies had the answer for transporting liquid fuel. **Flight Refuelling Ltd,** the company founded by Sir Alan Cobham, had a fleet of **Avro Lancasters** specially equipped for the purpose embodied in the company name; and to adapt these aircraft for tanker deliveries was a relatively straightforward task. The company carried more than 27,000 tons of petroleum fuel into Berlin—almost a third of the total.

Several other companies joined in with tanker aircraft, including **British South American Airways**, with **Tudors** (see p. 50). **Skyways** had 5 **Lancastrians**, **Airflight** supplied 2 Tudors and a **Lincoln**, while **Scottish Airlines** contributed two **Consolidated B-24 Liberators**. And the versatile **Haltons** (see p. 49) did their share of the liquid transport work.

These British independent operators carried all the liquid fuel: oil, gasoline, kerosene, and diesel (DERV).

Avro Lancaster, of Flight Refuelling, Ltd. (John Stroud Collection)

One of Skyways' Avro Lancastrians. (A.J. Jackson)

Airflight's Avro Lincoln, a developed version of the Lancaster.

... and Liberators

(B-24)

Payload 13,300 lb. ■ Speed 185 mph ■ Pratt & Whitney R-1830 Twin Wasp (1,200 hp) x 4 ■ Max. Gross Take-off Weight 60,000 lb. ■ Range 1,000 st. miles ■ Span 110 feet ■ Length 67 feet ■ Height 18 feet

A Lancashire Aircraft Corporation Halifax tanker takes on fuel for delivery to Berlin. (H.M.S.O.)

The Liquid Fuel Freighters Compared

Aircraft Type	Max. Dry Freight Load (lb)	Liquid Fuel (lb) Diesel	M.T. Gas	Kerosene
R.A.F. York	18,690	—	—	—
R.A.F. Hastings	19,000	—	—	—
Civil Tudor	20,600	17,950	17,447	17,950
Civil Lancastrian	—	18,698	17,853	18,237
Civil Lincoln	—	18,830	18,929	18,847
Civil Halifax/Halton	15,400	15,552	15,500	15,500
Civil York	20,500	—	—	—
USAF C-54	21,057	—	—	—

Source: Air Ministry Report on Operation Plainfare.

The Tanker Loads to Berlin

Airline	Aircraft No	Type	Tonnage
Airflight	2	Tudor	7,234
	1	Lincoln	426
B.A.A.S.	3	Halifax	3,938
B.S.A.A.	5	Tudor	19,813
Flight Refuelling	12	Lancastrian	27,115
Lancashire Aircraft Corp.	13	Halifax	15,198

Airline	Aircraft No	Type	Tonnage
Scottish Airlines	2	Liberator	2,716
Skyways	1	York	109
	5	Lancastrian	13,204
Westminster Airways	4	Halifax	2,592
TOTAL	46		92,345

Note: The numbers refer only to those aircraft carrying liquid fuel.

Passing the Salt

Short Sunderland

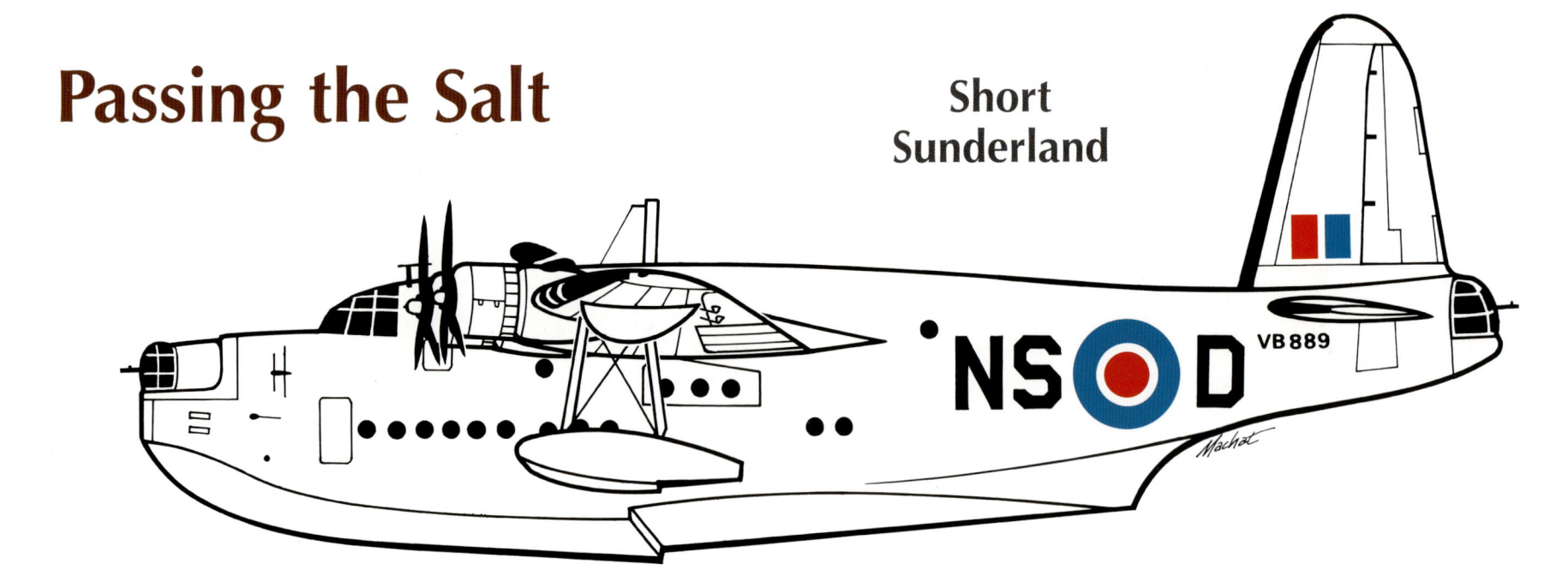

Payload 9,800 lb. ■ Speed 165 mph ■ Pratt & Whitney R-1830-90B Twin Wasp (1,200 hp) x 4 ■ Max. Gross Take-off Weight 65,000 lb. ■ Range 1,000 st. miles ■ Span 113 feet ■ Length 85 feet ■ Height 33 feet

Short Sunderland (civilian Hythe)

The Sunderland flying boat was used by the R.A.F. Coastal Command. The civilian firm Aquila Airways used the commercial version, called the Hythe. First developed in 1937, 792 of all variants were built, including the civil S-23s. The Sunderland provided the 38 tons of salt required each day in Berlin, as they were specially treated to resist corrosion (from sea water). They also transported manufactured goods and undernourished civilians out of Berlin in 1,000 trips, carrying 4,500 tons of supplies and over 1,113 children. The Sunderlands were first used during the Airlift on 2 July 1948, from Finkenwerder, near Hamburg. In December 1948, when Havel Lake froze, Halifax bombers were then assigned the task of transporting salt.

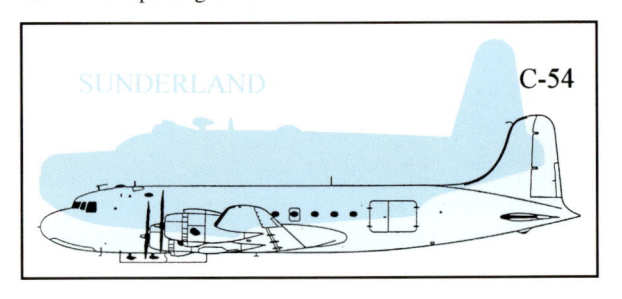

The Wannsee is a branch of the larger Havelsee, or Lake Havel, a widened section of the Havel River, a tributary of the Elbe. This aerial view, taken in 1948, shows two flying boats, one drawn up on the beach of the Wannsee, the other taxying on Lake Havel. (Photo by George Price)

The Ubiquitous DC-3

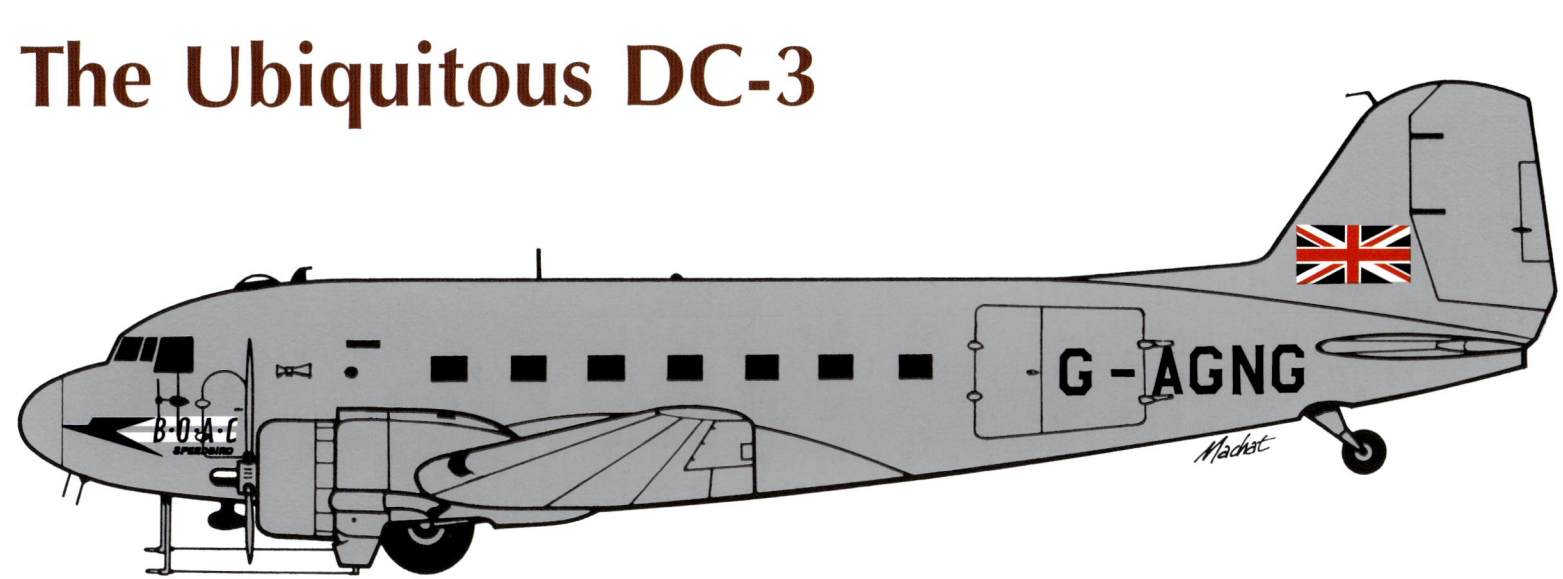

British Civil Dakota Tonnages

Airline	No	Tonnage
Air Contractors	3	1,377
Air Transport (C.I.)	1	743
B.N.A.S.	1	276
B.O.A.C.	3	294
Ciro's Aviation	2	1,177
Hornton	1	398
Kearsley Airways	2	889
Scottish Airlines	2	348
Sivewright Airways	1	116
Trent Valley Aviation	1	665
Westminster Airways	2	824
TOTAL	19	7,107

Payload 7,480 lb. ■ **Speed 150 mph** ■ **Pratt & Whitney R.1830 Twin Wasp (1,200 hp) x 2** ■ **Max. Gross Take-off Weight 31,000 lb.** ■ **Range 600 st. miles** ■ **Span 95 feet** ■ **Length 65 feet** ■ **Height 17 feet**
Note: Standard commercial (civilian) max. Gross Take-off Weight was 26,000 lb., standard payload was 6,000 lb.

Air Contractors sent 3 Dakotas to Germany for the Airlift and carried the most tonnage of all the civil C-47 operators.

The little-known (and short-lived) Ciro's Aviation ranked second of the British civil C-47 Airlift carriers.

G-AJZX of British Nederland Air Services.

G-AKLL of Hornton Airways.

G-AGWS of Scottish Airlines in flight is a reminder of the modest elegance of this almost indestructible design of the 1930 era. On one occasion a ground crew accidentally packed in a load allocated to an Avro York—which amounted to at least twice the certificated weight. The pilot thought that "she landed a bit heavy."

(All photos on this page: A.J. Jackson Collection)

55

Answering the Call
Bristol 170 Freighter Mk 21

Payload 8,700 lb. ■ **Bristol Hercules (1,700 hp) x 2** ■ **Max. Gross Take-off Weight 40,000 lb.** ■ **Span 108 feet** ■ **Length 68 feet**

British Charter Airlines

The R.A.F. alone, with other commitments overseas, could not achieve the required tonnage. Accordingly, the British Foreign Office chartered civilian carriers, contracted one month at a time, with a 14-day cancellation clause. 52 aircraft provided an additional 750 tons daily. 24 different charter airlines were under contract at one time or another to support the Airlift. On 1 April 1949, the **Civil Airlift Division** was formed, joining the Headquarters No. 46 Group at Lüneburg one month later. Many companies had been formed by young pilots, able to raise just enough money to buy the inexpensive military surplus aircraft.

British European Airways (B.E.A.) became the liaison in Germany, through which instructions and administrative duties were channelled. Mr. G.A.C.H. Foster was the liaison between civil companies and the R.A.F.. The latter did not supply spare parts or equipment and fuel or oil supplied had to be paid for, but the civilian companies had the use of hangars, workshops, battery-charging equipment, pre-heater vehicles, de-frosting vehicles, starter batteries, tractors, cranes, and other common aircraft equipment.

The short-term nature of these contracts prevented carriers from making large-scale investments, and some lacked experience for sustained operations, had inadequately trained pilots, and suffered from the general lack of spare parts. They were paid for flying time, depending on the type of aircraft used. By mid-August 1949, they were withdrawn from Airlift operations, by which time, however, they had transported 146,980 tons of supplies to Berlin. Many companies ceased operations shortly after the Airlift, as the nationalized state airlines left little commercial opportunities.

As illustrated above—and often forgotten in retrospect—is that the commercial airlines maintained scheduled services into Berlin in addition to the Airlift. The state airline, British European Airways (B.E.A.) operated from Bückeburg, near Hanover, and Hamburg.

Curiously, only one company (see table opposite) survives today, and it no longer operates aircraft. Kearsley Airways, still based at Stansted, near London, performs maintenance and other airport ground services.

Often regarded as an unattractive commercial airliner, the Avro Yorks of the R.A.F. did sterling Airlift work. 35 aircraft were deployed, each able to carry 8 1/2 tons (see page 51). (John Provan)

The Handley Page H.P. 67 Hastings arriving at Schleswigland on 1 November 1948. Powered by four Bristol Hercules engines, it had a maximum speed of 354 mph and a payload of 18,500 lb. The Hastings was 81 ft. 8 in. (24.9 m) long with a wingspan of 113 ft. (34.46 m). (John Provan)

The Spirit of Free Enterprise

Airline and Aircraft Type	Aircraft Regist.	Tonnage Carried Freight	Liquid Fuel
Air Contractors (Dakota)	G-AIWC G-AIWD G-AIWE	1,377	—
Airflight (Tudor)	G-AGRY G-AKBY	749	7,234
(Lincoln)	G-ALPF	7	426
Airwork (Bristol Freighter)	G-AHJD G-AICS	371	—
Air Transport (C.I.) (Dakota)	G-AJVZ	743	—
Aquila Airways (Hythe)	G-AGER G-AGIA G-AHED	1409	—
British American Air Services (Halifax)	G-AIAR G-AKBB G-AKGN	525	3,938
British Nederland Air Services (Dakota)	G-AJZX	276	—
British South American Airways (Tudor)	G-AGBZ G-AGRH G-AGRJ G-AKCA G-AKCB G-AKCC G-AKCD	2,312	19,813
British Overseas Airways Corp. (Dakota)	G-AGIZ G-AGNG G-AGNK	294	—
Bond Air Services (Halifax/Halton)	G-AHDN G-AHDO G-AHDP G-AHDS G-AHDT G-AHDU G-AHDW G-AHDX G-AIOI G-AIWN G-ALON G-ALOS	17,131	—
Ciro's Aviation (Dakota)	G-AIJD G-AKJN	1,177	—
Eagle Aviation (Halifax)	G-AIAP G-AIAR G-ALEF G-AJBL	7,304	—
Flight Refuelling (Lancastrian)	G-AGWI G-AGWL G-AHJU G-AHJW G-AHVN G-AKDO G-AKDP G-AKDR G-AKDS G-AKFF G-AKFG G-AKTB	—	27,115

Airline and Aircraft Type	Aircraft Regist.	Tonnage Carried Freight	Liquid Fuel
Hornton Airways (Dakota)	G-AKLL	398	
Kearsley Airways (Dakota)	G-AKAR G-AKDT	889	
Lancashire Aircraft Corporation (Halifax/Halton)	G-AHCX G-AHWN G-AHYH G-AIHV G-AIHY G-AILO G-AJZY G-AJZZ G-AKBJ G-AKBK G-AKEC G-AKXT G-ALBZ	1,215	15,198
Scottish Airlines (Dakota)	G-AGWS G-AGZF	348	—
(Liberator)	G-AHDY G-AHZP G-AHZR	110	2,717
Silver City Airways (Bristol Freighter)	G-AGVB G-AGVC	617	—
(Bristol Wayfarer)	G-AHJC G-AHJO	280	—
Sivewright Airways (Dakota)	G-AKAY	116	—
Skyflight (Halifax)	G-AIWP G-AKBR	276	—
Skyways (York)	G-ALBX G-AHFI G-AHLV	10,175	109
(Lancastrian)	G-AKBT G-AKFH G-AKMW G-AKSN G-AKSO	—	13,204
Transworld Charter (Vickers Viking)	G-AHON G-AHOT	415	—
Trent Valley Aviation (Dakota)	G-AJPF	665	—
World Air Freight (Halifax)	G-AKAC G-AKGZ G-AKTC	3,703	—
Westminster Airways (Dakota)	G-AJAY G-AJAZ	824	—
(Halifax)	G-AHDL G-AHDM G-AHDV G-AHNW	928	2,592
TOTAL	**104 aircraft**	**54,635**	**92,345**

Cometh the Hour . . .

The British charter airlines, deprived by legislation of the privilege of operating scheduled airline routes, came to the rescue when emergency additional capacity was required in 1948. They ranged from companies of some substance, such as Skyways, or Silver City Airways, and the specialist Flight Refuelling, to small, short-lived, opportunist enterprises. The biggest tonnage by a single airline was by Flight Refuelling (all liquid fuel), while the State corporation, British South American Airways and the independent Skyways were not far behind. But even Sivewright Airways' single Dakota pitched in, along with other long-forgotten contributors to the Allied effort.

The Vickers Viking was the British post-war answer to the Douglas DC-3. It was a derivative of the Wellington bomber, with a roomier fuselage than the DC-3's, and was used extensively by British airlines in the U.K. and the Commonwealth. (A.J. Jackson Collection)

Rather as the Fairchild C-82 was used by the U.S.A.F. for carrying awkward loads that needed very large doors, the Bristol Type 170 Freighter performed the same duties for the combined British contribution. (Bristol Aeroplane Co.)

The British Contribution — Summary

British Corridors
The British used their corridors somewhat differently. The U.S. Air Force used the southern and northern corridors flying towards Berlin and the central corridor only to return. The British used the northern corridor in both directions, returning to Hamburg or Schleswigland, while aircraft returning to other bases used the central corridor. To ensure safety, the corridors were divided into different altitudes, with the 3,000 ft. level empty for emergencies in most of them. The 1,000-1,500 ft. level was used for aircraft to and from Hamburg and Schleswigland. The 2,000-2,500 ft. level was reserved for eastbound Fassberg to Tegel, 3,000-3,500 ft. for eastbound Wunstorf to Gatow, 4,000-4,500 ft. for eastbound Celle to Gatow, and 5,000-5,500 ft. for aircraft to and from Lübeck-Gatow. The British usually kept aircraft at different heights, so that aircraft of different speeds would not collide in case of darkness or fog. (See pages 32–33, 47)

Poor weather, especially fog, often meant that groups of aircraft had to be diverted to other bases. The operation room maintained control even in the worst weather. Radio-controlled landings assisted in overcoming the weather, and the Frohnau radio beacon near Gatow was instrumental for air traffic control in the northern corridor. The Frohnau radio tower stood next to a church so the control tower at Gatow would often answer incoming aircraft with "O.K. Take a pew." Pilots called the tower the Christmas Tree, because of its red lights.

G.C.A.
The Ground Controlled Approach (G.C.A.) controller was in two trailers close to the runway (see page 47). On the radar screen could be seen the image of an aircraft and its exact relation to the runway it was approaching. The controller provided instructions to the pilot, as to altitude and direction, guiding him down through the fog. At the last moment, the pilot could see the runway lights and bring the aircraft down for a safe landing on his own. The controller would then begin assisting the next pilot on the screen. A series of cross-bar sodium approach lights were located at the center of the runway to assist pilots even in the worst weather. Later the same type of lights were also installed at the London airport. The development of G.C.A. would soon make civilian air transport much safer, although pilots were at first apprehensive about surrendering control to people on the ground.

British Dispatch Routine
Aircraft maintenance was generally handled by aircraft servicing companies in the United Kingdom. The British bases at Fassberg and Celle were later used by the U.S.A.F.. Each had two commanders, an American for operations, a Briton for administrative affairs.

The Combined Airlift Task Force Headquarters in Wiesbaden provided traffic flow into the Berlin airfields and coordinated the air traffic patterns. Procedures, principles of operation, and the Chain of Command were maintained separately by the U.S. and British forces.

British Air Freight
Operation Plainfare transported six general types of freight to Berlin. (1) 40 tons a day of food and supplies for British troops in Berlin. (2) 1,300 tons daily for the civilian population of West Berlin. (3) Coal for industrial use and domestic heating. (4) Liquid fuel, gasoline for motorized vehicles, diesel oil, etc. (5) Salt. (6) Special freight, such as newsprint (important for civilian morale), raw materials for Berlin industries, and miscellaneous goods, such as medicines, children's shoes, construction materials. The R.A.F. paid special attention to saving weight in packaging, avoiding tin cans, wooden boxes, and other heavy packaging. It was also responsible for transporting German civilian passengers. Adult German civilians paid a small fee, while children flew free of charge. Pilots always had some candy for the children. About 60,000 individuals were flown out, which also assisted in decreasing the number of hungry people in Berlin.

Something to Cheer About
Just as the American soldiers provided countless Christmas parties for the children of Berlin, so did members of the R.A.F. The British were surprised to find that many children were not familiar with chocolate, as they had never seen it. Twelve families of R.A.F. members were flown into Berlin as part of Operation Union, providing many a merry Christmas. On 23 December 1948, another record was set, the 50,000th Plainfare landing, when an R.A.F. aircraft landed at Gatow.

On 18 February 1949, the 1,000,000th ton of coal was transported in the combined Airlift. For this honor, lots were drawn and the R.A.F. won. A New Zealander was the pilot and the Commander-in-Chief (CinC) British Air Forces of Occupation was the co-pilot of a York aircraft which landed at Gatow. As the CinC stepped from his aircraft, he told the press, "It will not take us so long to reach the second million." The R.A.F. made a total of 87,841 flights in support of operations with the British peak occurring on 5 July 1949 with 2,314 tons of supplies airlifted on that day.

The G.C.A. Unit at Fassberg (Gloria Wenk)

U.S. Spirit of Competition

Howgozit
Tunner believed that, given the challenge of a good healthy competition, Americans can accomplish anything. This arose among the different Air Bases in the form of daily tonnage rates, especially between Fassberg versus Celle and Rhein-Main versus Wiesbaden. Large signs were erected at each base and daily tonnage figures noted, so that fliers could compare their achievements. The *Task Force Times* (see below), published these figures in a column called the Howgozit Board, usually on the front page. Rivalry between the Air Force and Navy also arose. Countless records were set by the U.S.A.F.E. and R.A.F.. The highest daily tonnages were 2,314 tons for the R.A.F., set on 5 July 1949, and 12,849 tons for U.S.A.F.E. set on 16 April 1949.

During Easter a quota had been set, far more than the tonnage of any previous day. This spurred the units to fill this quota, as a gift to the people of Berlin. On Easter Sunday; 1,398 flights were made, almost one for every 1,440 minutes in a day, without one accident or injury. This single day, remembered as the Easter Parade, may have broken the Berlin blockade, as daily tonnages would never fall below 9,000 again, far more than Berlin needed to survive.

The same spirit of competition arose among German civilians. Maintenance crews recorded the daily percentage of aircraft ready for duty. German workers noted the time required to load or unload an aircraft. One twelve-man German crew unloaded 20,000 lb. of coal in five minutes and 45 seconds. Each member of the crew was rewarded with a priceless pack of cigarettes.

The *Task Force Times*
The daily *Task Force Times*, produced at Wiesbaden A.B., was flown to Berlin, where departing aircraft would transport the papers to the other bases. Soviet agents in Berlin counted U.S. aircraft movements, which proved the tonnage figures to be correct and not just imperialistic propaganda. The staff were: 1st Lt. William G. Thompson (Public Information Officer, PIO), Pvt. Corbin Shuckahosee (distribution), TSgt. John Schuffert (cartoonist), Clarence T. Smith (editor), William Anderson (assistant PIO), PFC Preston Neuhard (production technician), Mary F. Harvey (assistant editor) and MSgt. Clyde Lother (NCOIC & staff writer). The paper ceased publication on 3 August 1949.

The competition helped to restore morale; because some resentment had set in when units were transferred to Germany from Texas, Panama, Hawaii, and Alaska on T.D.Y. (Temporary Duty), often for 30 to 90 days, then extended for 30 days, then another 30 days, and so on. One Navy unit had just been transferred to Hawaii and before the wives and children arrived, departed for Germany. Many would not see their families for almost a year.

Improvisation
Tunner would often fly the routes personally and visit the bases first hand. On one occasion, he invited thirty pilots to have a beer with him at his hotel, where after a stein or two, he questioned them about the changes he had made and whether they fulfilled their purpose or not. In his book *Over the Hump*, Tunner explained his style of management: "Making myself available to the pilots and crew members, seeking them out and listening to their complaints, gave me an insight into the true operations of the lift that I could never have gotten sitting at my desk reading filtered and secondhand reports. Frequently I learned of an accident before the commander of the base on which it had occurred."

"Don't do it by the book—improvise" was another Tunner motto. Group Captain Yarde, Commanding Officer at Gatow R.A.F. Air Base, had experienced landing problems because of numerous flocks of birds. He ordered a squadron of falcons from Malta, and within days of their arrival, the field was clear. At Wiesbaden A.B., a Sergeant equipped a truck with a jet-fighter engine, melting the ice from Airlift planes with the heat from the exhausts.

Open-air Vittles Howgozit board at Fassberg. Note that it was equipped with a light, for 24-hour inspection. (Albert Lowe)

American troops inspect the Howgozit Board at Rhein-Main. The spirit of competition was alive and well between squadrons from Alaska, Hawaii, Panama, and Texas. (U.S.A.F.)

The Human Touch

CARE...

An organization remembered by all, that is best summed up in one word, **CARE, Cooperative for American Remittances to Europe,** was created on 27 November 1945, by 22 religious, business and private aid groups. Six months later the first packages began arriving at Le Havre. Between 1946 and 1949, more than five million CARE packages were delivered to Germany alone, with more than 200,000 delivered to Berlin during the Airlift. A standard CARE package contained 29 lb. of dried eggs, powdered milk, flour, chocolate, and soap, which provided approximately 43,000 calories. These packages would cost donors $10, but packages to Berlin cost an additional $2.50 in air-freight charges. During the Airlift, pilots would drop 100 Shmoos (a small make-believe animal in the form of a balloon) on which a card was tied. Those who found Shmoos could take the card and obtain a CARE package. In some cases the donors designated the recipients by family name, and often gave descriptions such as a blue-eyed orphan boy, a needy paralytic, or the children's ward of a hospital. Commercial airlines such as **Seaboard & Western Airlines** and **A.O.A.** handled the task of transporting these packages independently of the U.S.A.F.E. Operation Vittles. A grateful German population still remembers the name CARE, and in turn created its own CARE organization in 1981 to assist other nations in need.

...and More

A large number of organizations, besides CARE, assisted during the Berlin Airlift, such as I.R.C. (International Red Cross), S.R.C. (Swiss Red Cross), B.H.A.C. (Berliner Hilfswerke, Aktionskomitee in Westdeutschland, Berlin Assistance, operating committee in West Germany), UNICEF (United Nations Children's Fund), A.F.S.C. (American Friends Service Committee- The Quakers), M.S.C. (Mennonite Assistance Committee), Catholic Relief Services, and the Church of Jesus Christ of Latter Day Saints (The Mormons). The A.F.S.C. was the first foreign welfare organization to undertake relief efforts in Berlin, with a center called Mittelhof, which opened in June 1947. A small organization, it is most remembered for providing oatmeal for children and temporary housing units for the homeless. The Mormons had large stockpiles maintained under a Church welfare program, and sent 6.6 million lb. of supplies to Germany between 1946 and 1950.

1,330,385 packages were delivered to Berlin alone; 739,304 from CARE, 394,519 from Caritas, 174,062 from S.R.C. and another 22,500 from the Netherlands Caritas, providing much needed relief to thousands of Germans. Between January 1946 and September 1949, these organizations provided 37,348,409 lb. of relief supplies to Berlin. Even during the blockade, these organizations generally divided their efforts: 36.6% to the Soviet sector, 30.5% to the American, 19.4% to the British and 13.5% to the French sectors.

The Soviets stopped a delivery of food for 20,000 needy children in all sectors of Berlin from the Swedish Red Cross. Sadly, this organization terminated its efforts under these conditions.

> The countless acts of humanitarianism are best symbolized in the story of a 13-year old (nameless) boy, who lived in Wiesbaden. The boy had just received word that his mother, who lived in Berlin, had suffered a heart attack and was very ill. He managed to pass the guards at the Air Base and made his way to an aircraft, when a pilot discovered him. He told his story to the pilot, who made sure no supervisors were watching, then lifted the lad into the aircraft and said, "Make yourself comfortable, son. In two hours you'll be in Berlin."

Project Sleighbells

Christmas 1948 was a special period. All over the world, dependents of those servicemen stationed in Germany during the Airlift gathered gifts for the children of Berlin. **Project Sleighbells,** was a great success, as was Operation Santa Claus from Fassberg A.B., U.S.A.F.E.

VR-6 and VR-8 held a Christmas party for the Steinheim Orphanage, near Frankfurt. Members of both units delivered a truck-load of toys and food to the orphanage on 22 December 1948. A Christmas play was then presented by 70 of the children for the servicemen.

The Soldier's Life

Dull Routine

While in Germany there was little to do other than work. Close fraternization with Germans, of both sexes, was taboo, at least officially. Fatigue was a major problem because of lack of sleep and overwork. Many crews used the auto-pilot, but this idea back-fired for one crew that did not wake up until they were over the English Channel. Airmen would suck dry Alka-Seltzer tablets or browse through girlie magazines, attempting to stay awake.

General Tunner once described life during the Airlift: "Pilots with their other crewmen flew this daily stint (to Berlin), night and day, and when finished went back to the crowded barracks or Quonset huts, heated with a smoking, dirty, pot-bellied, soft coal-burning stove."

During the early months of the Airlift, stress from overwork was a problem, for many, unpleasant family situations had been caused by the rapid deployment of their units. The lives of many military and dependents had been turned upside down. Capt. Clifford 'Ted' Harris, stationed on Johnston Island in the Pacific Ocean, recalls being located by a friend, John Campbell, who told him: "Ted, you've got to get yourself all together in thirty minutes. We're going to Berlin." Navy sailor William Glatiotis was having a beer in downtown Honolulu when a sergeant casually told him "Hey, Greek, you're shipping out in two hours' time."

The Chow Line was not up to Waldorf-Astoria standard. (U.S. Army Signal Corps)

Military officials tried to be generous with three-day passes and short vacations to Paris or Switzerland to make up for this life. The chaplains played an important role in the morale and welfare of the airmen, even though faced with a formidable task, for example at Rhein-Main A.B.. The number of personnel quickly rose from 2,000 to approximately 8,000, whereas the number of base chaplains increased from 2 to 3. They did a good job.

The medical staffs were deeply involved. Approximately 10 percent of the air crews were relieved of duty at any given time, because of sickness or injury, the majority during the cold winter months. The U.S.A.F. average for relatively inactive non-airlift bases was 2.5 percent. Airlifters could not always keep normal sick-call hours because their schedules did not match the daytime operating hours of medical personnel. The lack of hospital space often required patients to be referred to distant sites, increasing the length of sick leave. The American Red Cross handled more than 10,000 cases.

The accommodation also was not exactly 5-star. (U.S. Army Signal Corps)

The maintenance crews particularly, who had to be on call in all weathers, had to be close to the action, even in winter. (John Provan)

The Mobile Snack Bar must have been a welcome sight on the line of aircraft on the ramp. (Robert Pine)

61

Operation Little Vittles

Any Gum, Chum?
Among the more famous individuals who came forth from the Berlin Airlift was **1st Lt. Gail S. Halvorsen** who was born on 10 October 1920, in Salt Lake City. He began his military career in 1943, had served as a pilot in the South Atlantic, and in 1948 was assigned to Rhein-Main A.B. in connection with the Berlin Airlift. While piloting C-54s into Tempelhof, he met some German children standing along the fence of the base. The many years of war and hardship had left their mark. Gail had only two sticks of gum in his pocket, which he broke in two and gave to the children, telling them to share, but not nearly enough for all the children standing there. "For thirty cents, I could put these guys on Easy Street," he recalled. He told the children that he would fly into Berlin the next day and would drop candy (mainly chocolate) during his approach. The children asked "how will we recognize you?" Gail said he would tip his wings up and down, an old form of greeting among pilots.

Parachute Hankies
That night, he experimented with small parachutes made from handkerchiefs, which were in large supply to combat colds. Two pilots from the 17th Troop Carrier Squadron told Gail: "Better watch it, or they'll be shipping you back to the States." Gail answered jokingly: "Well, you know how easily a guy can get lift-happy." The next day, as he approached Tempelhof, he wiggled his wings and dropped several parachutes with candy attached. The kids went wild with joy, and every day more children would appear along the fence. The military learned of Gail's activity and at first was most displeased, as it had not been approved beforehand by the Chain of Command. On the other hand, these candy drops were a huge morale factor, not only for the German children, but for all the soldiers involved. From this humble beginning, **Operation Little Vittles** was created.

Production Line
Twenty-three tons of candy were collected by children from 22 schools in the Chicopee, Massachusetts, area, while member companies of the American Confectioners Assn., provided cord, sail cloth, and handkerchiefs. These goods were collected from several military installations, sent to Westover A.F.B. and then transported to Rhein-Main A.B., where the handkerchiefs became parachutes. According to the military (in a letter of regulations) these parachutes were to be made of lightweight cloth, 15 inches square, connected by four 16 inch-long pieces of string. The type of candy attached made no difference. Base units collected handkerchiefs and wives sewed mini-parachutes, often from surplus real ones. Inside the chutes was a note: "Please return this chute for re-use to the first M.P. you see." One M.P. at Rhein-Main A.B. gave Sgt. Vernon Earley a choice: a parking ticket or 70 cents worth of candy for Little Vittles. Even the Berliners were involved with this operation, collecting the used parachutes and bringing them back to Tempelhof, where they could be used again.

Children watch a C-54 on approach over the Berlin ruins, looking for the parachute hankies and the Hershey bars. (U.S.A.F.)

1st Lt. Gail S. Halvorsen, at the parachute-loading production line.

A Berlin youngster, at the parachute unloading end.

The Candy Bombers

Uncle Wiggly Wings
"Send in a handkerchief and we'll play your request tune" was provided by radio stations in the United States and soon five mail sacks a day were being delivered to Gail in support of his efforts. Thousands of letters of appreciation were sent to Gail, many often simply addressed to the **Candy Bomber**, the **Chocolate Pilot**, or **Uncle Wiggly Wings**. Even today Gail Halvorsen is remembered in the hearts of many Berliners. On 14 January 1949, he returned to the United States after serving in Germany for 7 months.

Eugene Williams Returns
Operation Little Vittles was continued by **Capt. Eugene T. Williams**, (also known as Willie) from Wiesbaden A.B., who was able to expand the project before the Airlift ended. For his actions, 1st Lt. Halvorsen received the Cheney Award in 1948 and later the German Bundes Verdienst Kreuz. His actions came to symbolize the good deeds that many pilots did during the Airlift. Gail would return to Germany, from 1962 to 1965, where he served at Wiesbaden A.B. and again to Berlin as Base Commander of Tempelhof A.B. from February 1970 to February 1974.

Williams completed his final bombing raid, on 15 September 1949, when a B-17 Flying Fortress flew twice over Moosburg, a small town, dropping thousands of candy bars, each tied to a small parachute. 1st Lt. Harry W. Bachus, who piloted the B-17, knew Moosburg well. He had been a prisoner of war there for five long months.

No caption is needed for this picture (and no commercial advertisement either).

Thousands of candy bars go overboard over Berlin, helped on their way by a securely-roped-in Candy Bomber, 1st Class, Eugene Williams. (U.S.A.F.)

63

The Lighter Side

Both the multi-colored fuselage titles and the camel were hastily hand-painted. The term "Camel Caravan" was the name of a popular radio show, featuring the swing bands of the era, and sponsored by a well known brand of cigarettes.

Clarence
The operation also had its amusing side. On 21 October 1948, **Clarence** (a camel) along with 5,000 pounds of candy were flown into Berlin, to the cheers of more than 5,000 children. The baby camel was the mascot of the 525th Fighter Squadron, stationed at Neubiberg A.B., Germany. The unit had deployed to Tripoli, Libya, for bombing practice, where 1st Lt. Don Butterfield had been offered the animal for $50. After the blockade began, unit members decided that Clarence was just what the children needed, so he was flown to Berlin to do his best to provide what cheer a camel could.

That's Entertainment
Special Services Division, Headquarters U.S.A.F. arranged entertainment productions and sent them to Europe in support of the Berlin airlift. **Edgar Bergen**, along with his puppets Charlie and Mortimer gave a memorable show at the Rhein-Main "Country Club" on 25 July 1948. American gold medal winners of the Olympic Games, held in London in 1948, made a stopover at Rhein-Main A.B. before heading home.

Christmas Caravan
This starred **Bob Hope**, **Irving Berlin** (who wrote a special song about the Airlift) and **Jane Russell**, along with 34 other celebrities, arrived in Europe on 21 December 1948, and in the following 10 days gave shows in Wiesbaden, Rhein-Main, Berlin, Fassberg, and Burtonwood, England. Vice-President Alben W. Barkley and Secretary of the Air Force W. Stuart Symington accompanied the show.

The soldiers at Rhein-Main A.B. waited patiently in the bitter cold on 28 December 1948. Standing outside the newly built movie theater, they gathered Christmas trees and burned them to keep warm. Bob Hope entered the theater with a parachute; he pulled the rip cord only to find the chute filled with cartons of cigarettes. Cigarettes were strictly rationed at the time, one carton per soldier per week at $1.00. On the black market a carton of cigarettes was worth 140 DM ($35) and many soldiers paid their rent with one carton a month. The military police watched to be sure that no cigarettes would be stolen. Bob remarked about the bad weather during the Airlift, "Soup I can take—but this stuff's got noodles in it!" a statement that most pilots could agree with.

The **Special Services Section, C.A.L.T.F.**, drew upon the talents of Airlift personnel and their dependents to create soldier shows, such as **Vittles Varieties** which then toured other bases, providing much needed entertainment. Garry Moore and his NBC show **Take It or Leave It**, toured bases in February 1949. Connie Bennett and her show **Over 21**, starred on many base stages during April 1949. By July 1949, the Airlift had slowed down enough for 20th Century-Fox to produce a film entitled **Quartered City** (later renamed the **Big Lift**) at a former German studio near Tempelhof. Many airmen stationed at Rhein-Main A.B. played a role in the film as extras.

A.F.N. – Armed Forces Network
The Armed Forces Network (A.F.N.) radio station played a significant role during the Berlin Airlift. Its network of radio stations in Germany had been created to provide American soldiers with the latest news and music from back home. **A.F.N. Berlin** operated 18 hours a day from its studios in a exclusive villa of a former Berlin banker at No. 28 Podbielskiallee. When the blockade occurred, the German population was extremely nervous and uncertain if U.S. soldiers would remain in the city. A.F.N. immediately began broadcasting 24 hours a day, as a symbol of America's resolve. Weary crews often kept awake by listening and used the station as a homing device while flying into Berlin. A.F.N. Berlin was a major morale booster for the citizens of Berlin as well. **A.F.N. Frankfurt**, located in the romantic medieval castle at Höchst, provided the Rhein-Main and Wiesbaden areas with the badly needed entertainment and information, while reporters were often on board aircraft as passengers, flying back and forth, to produce many an interesting story of the Airlift.

"I'LL CALL YOUR TWO SACKS OF COAL AND RAISE YOU THREE BAGS OF FLOUR!"

Airlift Laffs

On the Lighter Side

The lighter side of the Airlift was presented in cartoons depicting the daily events. **TSgt Jack (Jake) Schuffert** had joined the military in 1941 and decorated airplanes with cartoons and nose-art. He was later assigned to General Tunner's crew as radio operator and was able to visit the different bases. His cartoons soon began to appear in the *Stars and Stripes*, the Rhein-Main AB Gateway paper, and later in the *Task Force Times*. "Jake had an extraordinary knack of giving his readers just what they wanted to see," wrote General Tunner. "His cartoons were raw and bitter and played up everything disagreeable on the Airlift, but they brought a smile to their readers faces..." A booklet of his best jokes was published and called *Airlift Laffs*.

"Yeah, all the way from Great Falls in these damn bucket seats."

Tunner recalled one conversation with a pilot, who had just landed his C-54 filled with coal, his 210th flight during the Airlift. The pilot was dirty and tired and looked more like a coal miner than an Air Force pilot. He said: "You know, General, there's one thing we can be thankful for in hauling all this coal to Berlin." "Yes" Tunner said, "What's that?" "At least we don't have to haul out the ashes."

"OH BOY, LOOKS LIKE THE WEATHER IN BERLIN IS REALLY BAD TODAY."

"WILL YOU PLEASE REPEAT THAT LAST TRANSMISSION!"

"HEY, WAIT A MINUTE, THAT'S CARRYING THIS AIRLIFT THING A BIT TOO FAR."

"JUST OUR LUCK; A COTTONPICKIN' COAL PLANE!"

The Darker Side

Calculated Risk
Inevitably, in an operation that had to be initiated at short notice, the preparations for a concentrated program of flights, on several different routes, with inadequate navigational aids, were fraught with danger. Risks had to be taken, if the Airlift was to achieve the necessary volume and momentum. Such risks were quickly evident, when a C-54 crashed during only the second week; and a C-47 crashed dramatically, and tragically, at its destination in Berlin. In the second month, two C-47s collided in mid-air, during heavy fog (even in the summer). The need for strict operational discipline was quickly apparent.

Safety, with an Occasional Accident
Good maintenance resulted in fewer accidents. Therefore, Tunner's determination for safety played an important factor in the Airlift. Worldwide, the U.S.A.F. had 48 accidents per 100,000 flying hours in July 1948, while for the Berlin Airlift the rate was only 39. Even during the bad weather of December and January, the rates were 61 and 67 worldwide, yet only 43 and 30 respectively in Germany. A total of 50 minor and 76 major accidents occurred during the Berlin Airlift, of which 32 occurred during taxying and 37 while on approach and landing. The U.S. civilian carriers suffered no known accidents.

Other Incidents
On 2 October 1948, PFC Johnnie T. Orms had just completed fighting a brush fire at the end of the runway at Rhein-Main A.B. Afterwards, he drove his fire truck down the taxiway, into the sunlight, when at the same time a block of C-54s was taxying to the east. Blinded by the sunlight and landing lights from the aircraft, PFC Orms was killed instantly, when the cabin of the truck was torn apart by one of the engines from the on-coming aircraft.

Not all crashes were fatal. A C-47, commanded by Capt. Kenneth W. Slaker and Lt. Clarence Steber, was flying from Wiesbaden to Berlin, on 14 September 1948, when suddenly both engines stopped after entering the Soviet Zone. Both men bailed out of the aircraft. The Soviet military picked up Lt. Steber and turned him over to the U.S. military authorities, while Capt. Slaker simply walked back through the Iron Curtain, with the assistance of some friendly East Germans.

On 15 November 1948, a Navy R5D, tail number 56545, coming from Rhein-Main, overshot the runway at Tempelhof, crashed and burned. ADC Sidney D. Pointer received a letter of commendation, personally written by General Clay, for his rescue work in saving the life of U.S.A.F. Capt. Armand I. Grenadier who was on board this aircraft.

The Record, in Perspective
One journalist summed up the accident figures and safety record. "Why, I'm safer on the Berlin Airlift than I am flying between Washington and New York." In almost 300,000 flights, in testing operational circumstances, only 22 accidents occurred. And, as with many accidents, lessons were learned, and the concentration of effort during the Berlin Airlift paid handsome dividends throughout armed forces aviation everywhere in the years to come.

AIRLIFT CASUALTIES

Date	Aircraft	Location	Fatalities
8 July 48	C-54	Königstein	1st Lt George B. Smith 1st Lt Leland V. Williams Karl v. Hagen (Dept. of Army)
25 July 48	C-47	Berlin	1st Lt Charles H. King 1st Lt Robert W. Stuber
24 Aug 48	C-47(2)	Ravolzhausen	Maj. Edwin C. Diltz Capt. Willaim R. Howard Capt. Joel M. DeVolentine 1st Lt. William T. Lucas
18 Oct 48	C-54	Rhein-Main	Capt. James A Vaughan 1st Lt Eugene Erickson Sgt. Richard Winter
5 Dec 48	C-54	Fassberg	Capt. Billy E. Phelps 1st Lt. Willis F. Hargis TSgt. Lloyd C. Wells
8 Dec 48	R5D	Taunus Mtns	AMM3 Harry R. Crites Jr.
7 Jan 49	C-54	Burtonwood	1st Lt Lowell A. Wheaton, Jr. 1st Lt Richard M Wurgel Capt. William A. Rathgeber Sgt. Bernhard J. Watkins Cpl. Norbert H. Thies Pvt. Ronald E. Stone
12 Jan 49	C-54	Rhein-Main	1st Lt. Ralph H. Boyd 1st Lt. Craig B. Ladd TSgt Charles L. Putnam
18 Jan 49	C-54	Fassberg	1st Lt. Robert P. Weaver
4 Mar 49	C-54	Fulda	1st Lt. Royce C. Stephens
12 July 49	C-54	Rathenow	2nd Lt. Donald J. Leemon 1st Lt. Robert C. von Leuhrte TSgt Herbert F. Heinig

British Problems

The Proximity Factor

Of the five accidents sustained by the Royal Air Force, three occurred near Lübeck. This circumstance was noteworthy in that the airfield was only a few miles from the western frontier of the Russian Zone of Occupation.

A most tragic accident occurred on 17 November 1948, when nine Dakotas from No. 30 Squadron were returning from Berlin. One aircraft, a Dakota, (K.P. 223), was piloted by F.I. Trezona, and he was the only pilot among the group without an instrument rating. His aircraft was in the middle of the eight other planes. The weather had deteriorated at Lübeck, while on approach. After the first had landed, contact was suddenly lost with Trezona. The next aircraft noted a fire below in the Russian Zone. The next day Squadron Leader Johnstone (the same pilot who first flew into Tegel), failed to obtain permission from the Soviet authorities to enter their Zone. He began searching from the air, failing to locate the crash site. The Russians claimed to have found the remains of the victims, Trezona, Sgt. F. Dowling and S3 P.A. Lough and one badly injured survivor, who was being hospitalized. Flt. Lt. J.G. Wilkins, navigator, died later in the hospital in Schöneberg. Unknown to the ground control, the pilot, F.I. Trezona, had allowed Lough to come along as a passenger, as he was on leave for humanitarian reasons. The political and military situation became very tense. Had the Russians shot the aircraft down? Or was this the beginning of a general offensive? This uncertain situation was prolonged with the accidents on 24 January and 22 March 1949.

The accident on 24 January 1949 was also very tragic. A Royal Air Force Dakota (K.P. 491) was piloted by E.J. Eddy on a flight to Lübeck, along with L. Senior (Navigator) and L.E. Grout (Signaller) as crew. On board were 22 German passengers, mainly children. The weather was turbulent and while on approach, the aircraft crashed in the Russian Zone, and was torn into two sections. R.A.F. member E. Grout and seven passengers were killed. Nine passengers were released by the Soviets on 27 January, with the remaining crew and passengers following when they had recovered enough from their injuries to travel.

Not all the accidents were fatal, 10 May 1949, a Lancastrian (G-AKDP) crashed, injuring four; 12 June 1949, a Halton (G-ALBZ) crashed, injuring one; and 26 June 1949, a Lancastrian (G-AKFH) crashed, injuring three of the crew.

On one occasion, a German truck driver collided with the wing of a taxying Dakota, the driver protesting that the aircraft was flying much too low.

On 11 March 1949, a German policeman (name unknown) was killed when he walked during the night into the propeller of a York (M.W. 189) at Gatow.

These were the remains of a U.S. C-47, carrying food, when it crashed into a city street in Berlin, Friedenau, on 25 July 1948 (see table on opposite page). Several mayors were present at memorial ceremonies, and thousands of letters of condolence were received from Berlin citizens. (U.S.A.F.)

ROYAL AIR FORCE CRASHES

Date	Aircraft	Location	Fatalities
19 Sept 48	York	Wunstorf	Flt. Lt. H. W. Thomson Flt. Lt. G. Kell Nav. II L. E. H. Gilbert Sig. II S. M. L. Towersey Eng. II E. W. Watson
17 Nov 48	Dakota	near Lübeck	F.I. Trezona Sgt. F. Dowling S3 P. A. Lough (passenger) Flt. Lt. J. G. Wilkins
24 Jan 49	Dakota	near Lübeck	E. Grout 7 passengers
22 March 49	Dakota	near Lübeck	Flt. Lt. M. J. Quinn Nav. K. A. Reeves Sig. A. Penny
16 July 49	Hastings	Tegel, Berlin	Flt. Off. I. R. Donaldson Sgt. J. Toal Nav. I W. G. Page Sig. II A. Dunshire Eng. II R. R. Gibbs

BRITISH CIVIL CONTRACTOR ACCIDENTS

Date	Aircraft	Company	Location	Fatalities
23 Nov 48	Lancastrian	Flight Refuelling	Thruxton, England	Capt. Cyril Taylor Capt. Reg. M. W. Heath Capt. William Cusack Nav. Off. Michael E. Casey Nav. Off. Alan J. Burton Rad. Off. D. W. Robertson Flt. Eng. Kenneth Seaborne
8 Dec 48	Tudor	Airflight	Gatow, Berlin	Capt. Clement W. Utting
15 March 49	York	Skyways		Capt. Cecil Golding 1st Off. Henry T. Newmann Radio Off. Peter J. Edwards
21 March 49	Halifax	Lancashire Aircraft Corp.	Jagel	Capt. Robert J. Freight Nav. James P. L. Sharp Flt. Eng. Henry Patterson
30 April 49	Halifax/Halton	World Air Freight		Capt. Wm. R. D. Lewis Nav. Off. Ed. E. Carroll Eng. Off. John Anderson Rad. Off. Kenneth G. Wood

Armed Forces Cooperation

The Ground Work
The point has been emphasized (see page 41) that "90% of aviation is on the ground." And this axiom applied not only to the maintenance, but also to the considerable effort that had to be made in loading and unloading the aircraft, to a severely demanding schedule, and almost all of it by strong-armed men who, in 1948, were ill-equipped or provided for by what today would be standard mechanical equipment. There was hardly a fork-lift vehicle to be seen. It was all done by the sweat of the brow, alternatively begrimed by coal dust or flour dust, or in the British sector, caked in salt or impregnated with petroleum.

U.S. Army Support
The **U.S. Army Europe** played an essential role in supporting the Airlift, by at first handling and transporting supplies from the railhead to the airplane and in Berlin. At the Airlift Task Force headquarters in Wiesbaden, an Army liaison team coordinated the responsibilities.. Later, the U.S. Army Airlift Support Command (USAASC) was created, consolidating all Army activities under one commander, **Gen. Philip E. Gallagher**, with headquarters in Frankfurt.

A total of 1,904 U.S. Army personnel were engaged in Airlift support by March 1949. It organized nine companies of displaced Germans to provide manpower, mainly at Rhein-Main and Wiesbaden. Workers were housed in camps in Eschborn, Zeilsheim, and Zeppelinheim. The 66th, 67th, 68th, 69th, 70th, 76th, 83rd and 84th Transportation Truck Companies (Heavy) were assigned to Airlift support, each unit having 48 tractors and 96 trailers. The units were primarily staffed by black soldiers, as the desegregation of the military was still in its earliest stages. They were assigned to the **24th Transportation Truck Battalion**, which controlled all truck operations at Rhein-Main and Wiesbaden. The Army also provided and maintained more than 1,000 vehicles. Here too, spare parts and maintenance became a major problem. Most maintenance work was handled by the **559th Ordnance Company** at shops located at Rhein-Main A.B.

More important, the Army also supplied more than 500,000 duffel bags, badly needed to transport coal inside aircraft. By 1 March 1949, these were replaced by 1,716,000 cloth sacks and by May, paper sacks were put into use.

The **Army Quartermaster** provided subsistence, equipment, and clothing for Airlift personnel, especially for those stationed at Celle and Fassberg A.B.. This included laundry service, petroleum products and building materials. The 2905th, 2958th, 4052nd, 4060th, 4543rd, 7441st, 8512th, 8957th Labor Service Companies were assigned to the Quartermaster to support the Airlift, and mainly comprised civilians from many nationalities.

The Army's **862nd Engineer Aviation Battalion** (with the support of a Polish Refugee Unit—the 7,329th Labor Service Unit) and the 831st Engineer Aviation Battalion, provided engineering support and construction at most of the U.S.A.F. airfields involved in the Airlift. These units built the runways, erected the barracks, and provided the infrastructure necessary to maintain the large scale operations. Army and Air Force personnel worked together in each unit.

The Army Transportation Division also coordinated rail service with the German authorities. Extra baggage cars were added to trains running between Fassberg and Erding, providing fast movement of parts, supplies and cargo. A daily train also connected Frankfurt to Celle and Fassberg, beginning in December 1948.

The US Navy's Role
The U.S. Navy also played a vital role, operating two Naval Transport Squadrons from Rhein-Main A.B. Each squadron maintained twelve R5D (Naval version of the C-54 or DC-4). **VR-6** Squadron was attached to the 513th Troop Carrier Group and **VR-8** to the 61st Troop Carrier Group. The Air Force had 250 men in any given Squadron, while the Navy had 400 who proved to be as self-contained, and efficient. The Navy units maintained a much larger inventory of spare parts and supplies, and occupied its own section at Rhein-Main A.B., made up of 30 Quonset hut barracks and one Mess Hall. The 200-hour flight inspections of Navy aircraft were handled after 24 December 1948 at Rhein-Main A.B., rather than at Burtonwood, when the move had been completed.

In their eight months in Germany, VR-6 and VR-8 flew 45,900 hours, carrying 130,000 tons of cargo to Berlin. Navy Cdr. Charles J. Eastman received the meritorious achievement award for flying 134 round trips between 4 January and 9 May 1949.

These oil drums, laid out in thousands at Rhein-Main, Frankfurt, contained some of the 3 million gallons of high-octane fuel that was used up every month. This was quite separate from the supply of gasoline, kerosene, and fuel oil airlifted into Berlin by the British tanker aircraft. (U.S. Army Signal Corps)

This corner of the rail depot at Zeppelinheim, near Frankfurt, provides a small glimpse of the organization required of the ground transport sector of the Airlift. Hundreds of trucks transferred supplies from the freight trains to the airfield ramps. In the picture two can be seen unloading from the freight cars.

Vittles Statistics

Women in the Airlift
Very few women served in the military during the Berlin Airlift. The first was Navy Lt. Margaret E. Carver, assigned as personnel officer for VR-8 at Rhein-Main A.B. in December 1948. Capt. Kathryn M. Ludiow was the first WAF (Women in the Air Force) assigned to the Airlift, as personnel officer for the 61st Air Base Group on 1 April 1949. She was the first WAF assigned to the base, while several more served at Rhein-Main during the latter stage of the Airlift. Women assisted as personnel officers, special services representatives, or as Red Cross volunteers.

Logistics
The Berlin Airlift was a logistics problem of huge dimensions. More than 100,000,000 gallons of aviation fuel were delivered to Bremerhaven by U.S. Navy tanker ships—**U.S. Navy Sea Lift**, then piped or shipped by rail to the different airfields in time to meet daily requirements. Rhein-Main A.B. alone required more than 3 million gallons of high-octane fuel every month.

Spare engines were airlifted from Kelly A.F.B. to Rhein-Main A.B. in the large C-74 Globemaster I, which could carry 14 engines on a single flight. To improve the electricity supply, the rebuilding of the large power station required bulky and heavy machinery to be airlifted.

It was more efficient to transport flour and coal than baked loaves of bread (which contain 30% water). Real coffee was cheaper than providing fuel for the manufacture of ersatz coffee (replacement coffee). Berliners were now able to drink real coffee. Every item airlifted was considered in terms of economic and social effects, consumption of fuel, and morale.

Costs
The U.S. Air Force carried 1,421,730 tons of coal, 296,303 tons of food and 65,540 tons of miscellaneous items to Berlin, a total of 1,783,573 tons. The total cost of the Berlin Airlift was $137,177,427.00 broken down as follows:

Depreciation & Depot Maintenance	28.72%	Flight Maintenance	6.35%
Fuel & Lubricants	21.07%	Field Aircraft Maintenance	4.34%
Flight Personnel	11.34%	Flight Service	4.17%
Administrative Overhead	10.30%	Automotive Vehicles	2.09%
Subsistence Undistr. charges	9.11%	Air Installations & Construction Costs	2.51%

Cost analysis showed a great saving in maintenance personnel, aircrews, numbers and fuel by using larger aircraft. The C-54 was more economical than the C-47, and the new C-74 would have been even more economical. Individual base costs were:

Base	Cost	Base	Cost
Rhein-Main AB	$45,726,874.00	HQ ALTF	$9,114,899.00
Fassberg AB	$17,030,090.00	Tempelhof AB	$5,222,832.00
Wiesbaden AB	$13,666,134.00	Erding	$ 037,034.00
Celle AB	$10,613,796.00	Oberpfaffenhofen	$1,267,035.00
Burtonwood	$10,010,823.00		
	non-U.S.A.F.E.)	Total	$116,689,517.00

U.S. Military Units
The following U.S. Air Force units participated in the Berlin Airlift:

Wiesbaden

60th Troop Carrier Group: 10th, 11th 12th and 333rd Troop Carrier Squadrons
317th Troop Carrier Group: 22nd, 39th, 40th, 41st Troop Carrier Squadrons (later moved to Celle)
7120th Air Base Group
7196th Weather Reconnaissance Squadron
1420th Air Transport Group (Provisional)
1422nd Air Transport Group: 1st and 3rd Air Transport Squadrons

Rhein-Main

61st Troop Carrier Group: 14th, 15th, 17th and 53rd Troop Carrier Squadrons, VR-8 Naval Transport Squadron
513th Troop Carrier Group: 330th, 331st and 332nd Troop Carrier Squadrons, VR-6 Naval Transport Squadron
1422nd Air Transport Group: 8th, 9th, 11th, 12th, 21st, 22nd, 1250th, 1251st, 1255th and 1267th Air Transport Squadrons
19th Troop Carrier Squadron (Hickam Field, Honolulu)
20th Troop Carrier Squadron (Panama)

Fassberg

1420 Air Transport Group: 1256th, 1263rd, 1268th, 1773rd Air Transport Squadrons
54th Troop Carrier Squadron (Anchorage, Alaska)
313th Troop Carrier Group: 11th, 29th, 47th and 48th Troop Carrier Squadrons
513th Troop Carrier Group: 513th Supply Squadron
513th Maintenance Squadron
7496th Air Wing: 7497th Supply Squadron
7498th Base Service Group

Celle

7480th Air Force Wing
317th Troop Carrier Wing (Moved from Wiesbaden, on December 16, 1948)

Tempelhof

7350th Air Base Group:

Gatow

Gatow Detachment, 7350th Air Base Group

Tegel

Tegel Detachment, 7350th Air Base Group

69

The Siege and the Berliners

Ernst Reuter Mobilizes
German civilians contributed to the Berlin Airlift. Ernst Reuter (see page 11), the elected mayor of West Berlin, mobilized public support. Berliners worked hard to support the Allied activities: A runway at Tegel was constructed in only 62 days. They worked around the clock to improve Tempelhof and Gatow airfields, built the electric power plant (Kraftwerk West) and established the Free University of Berlin. Most of the loading and unloading was done by German nationals. Although food, fuel, and power were in short supply, Berlin was able to keep its industry going. The Allies had been considered a Besatzungsmacht (army of occupation) before the Airlift, now it seemed to be a Schutzmacht (army of protection).

Reuter had formerly been in charge of transport and public utilities and was able to smuggle out blueprints of the city's water, gas, sewage, and streetcar systems from the eastern sector of Berlin. These plans were essential to General Clay during the Airlift, for local distribution of supplies from the airfields.

Rationing
While in western Germany, conditions were improving, including better food supplies, the reverse was happening in Berlin. One Berliner stated it simply: "We blockaded Berliners aren't starving, but we're always hungry." The average daily ration consisted of: 15 ounces bread, 1.5 oz. sugar, 1.75 oz. prepared foods, 15oz. dried potatoes, 1.5 oz. meat, 0.175 oz. cheese, 1oz. fats.

This was still high compared to the situation directly after World War Two. One small contribution was 942 tons of Soviet-owned flour, discovered in a warehouse. For the entire winter of 1948–49, only 27.5 lb. of heating fuel (wood, coal, etc.) were available to each Berliner. However, the number of civilian deaths attributed to malnourishment or extreme cold was negligible, despite the food rationing. On the political front, on 9 September 1948, more than 300,000 people demonstrated against the blockade.

The creative and inventive nature of a people during hard times came forth among Berliners. Oil lamps were discovered in attics and repaired. Every possible item of use was uncovered and used again. Replacement parts were crafted. People built home-made, hand-operated generators that provided additional power. Throughout the city, Blockade Gardens were planted. Flower boxes filled entire balconies with growing fruits, potatoes, and vegetables. These crops provided several thousand tons of food.

Vitamin deficiencies were fought by tablets, especially vitamin C, still stockpiled from the war, twelve tablets a month. 45 tons of medical supplies were airlifted in each month. 1,500 tuberculosis cases were airlifted by the U.S.A.F.E. to sanitaria in western Germany. 15,426 children were flown out, to other homes for better nutrition and warmth,. 7,923 in the British, 6,535 in the American, and 968 in the French Zones. The first group returned home on 22 May 1949. Amazingly no epidemics occurred and no dramatic increase in death caused by diseases was noted during the Airlift period.

To help fight the cold, huge amounts of clothing were airlifted to Berlin. Half a million pieces of clothing and 10,000 tons of packages of donated clothing were flown into the city, with a total value of more than 50 million D-Marks. At Christmas 1948 and Easter 1949, every Berliner received an additional 100 grams of chocolate and adults 25 grams of coffee. The tough times were made bearable.

"Give us This Day our Daily Bread." The Allies quickly realized that to airlift baked bread was wasteful in terms of volumetric capacity in the aircraft; and so the basic ingredient, flour, was brought in by the sackful (top). This was baked in Berlin (center), and then sold in the shops, strictly rationed, as emphasized in the notice. (Top picture U.S.A.F.; lower pictures U.S. Army Signal Corps)

A child wrote: "Dear mother. As we departed you became smaller and smaller, and then I could not see you at all. We flew in the cloud, high in the skies. I wish we could stay an entire year up so high, it was wonderful. Every morning, we receive milk and eggs for breakfast. I am allowed to pick out the eggs myself from the chicken pen. I know each cow and pig, one I call Lottchen. When I return, you won't recognize me, I have gained much weight and am much stronger."

Sticking It Out

Employment
The Allies tried to maintain the industries of Berlin to ensure employment. Items produced in Berlin received a marking: "Hergestellt im Blockierten Berlin" (Produced in Blockaded Berlin). The Siemens factory exported by air 600 telephones per week, as well as other electrical goods. During the Airlift, 18,050 tons of manufactured goods were flown out, representing an average value of more than $4,151,200 per month, as well as 17,725 tons of mail.

Many Germans were employed by the Allies at the airfields. Even white-collar workers handled the hard physical work well. This employment meant a good ration card and a hot midday meal, although the pay was only 1.20 DM per hour and in shifts around the clock.

The majority of loading and unloading was handled by hired displaced persons, refugees or Germans. "Most of the half million or so tons flown to Berlin during 1948 travelled part of the way on a man's back." Equipment did not exist that could maneuver inside a plane, and the critical shortage of available time created the huge demand for manpower. The 8958th Labor Service Company, composed of Polish refugees, started work on 30 June 1948. Soon the 1839th, 2905th (German), 2958th, 4052nd, 4060th, 4543rd (Polish), 7441st (German), 8512th (Polish), 8957th and 8958th Labor Service Companies joined the Airlift. Approximately 7,100 laborers worked 12 hours on, 24 hours off, with one day off per week. Hard physical work was done by everyone. Many women removed rubble from the city of Berlin, which amounted to 800,000 cubic meters of earth, 420,000 cubic meters of brick, and 30,000 tons of tar.

Tragedy
Civilian casualties also occurred. Kurt Felgentreff witnessed one man accidentally fall into a rock crusher. Another man fell to his death into a large boiling pot of asphalt. Work on the runway stopped for a moment, but winter was approaching and the line moved on. Nine Germans were killed as a direct result of working on the Airlift.

Save the Trees!
Berlin was proud of its trees, which had survived the war, and amidst the ruins, the trees provided a symbol of comfort and hope. The military recommended cutting 350,000 meters of wood. Civilian officials suggested cutting only 120,000 meters, and dependent on how severe the upcoming winter would be, the rest of the trees could be cut if required. The winter was mild, and Berliners kept their trees. The Soviets reacted to this proposed deforestation program by announcing in the papers; Berlin Loses its Beauty.

Firewood Fatigue
Mothers with a special permit were allowed to collect wood scraps and roots during the day for heating at night. An official once reported: It takes five hours to dig out 60 pounds of tree roots, another six hours to cut them into small usable pieces. 72 hours were required to dry the roots, before one could use it and then it would only supply 8 hours of heat. At Christmas time, every family received a small bundle of fresh cut firewood, which caused much smoke and smell, but provided some heat for the holidays. The state of Schleswig-Holstein sent 2 million pine tree seedlings, each one inch long, to begin replanting even during the blockade. After the blockade and as part of the Marshall Plan, a large-scale program, replanting several hundred thousand trees, would return this beauty to the city in years to come.

Power Supplies
Electric power was a major problem. The Soviets had dismantled the large Kraftwerk West (Powerplant West) before the British took over. Three-quarters of Berlin's electricity was supplied by power plants in the Soviet sector. During the Airlift, power was rationed to portions of the city, twice daily for two hours. 875,000 kilowatts (kW) of power were produced daily, with 165,000 kW for Berlin's industry, 140,000 kW for households, 90,000 kW for transportation, and only 4,000 kW for street lighting. Equipment for rebuilding the Kraftwerk West was airlifted in, often in C-82s, and portable generators provided hospitals with electric power 24 hours a day.

King Coal
Coal was the main supply of heat, and strictly rationed. Most offices, factories or jails, received no coal for heating purposes. Hospitals were allowed coal to maintain a minimum temperature. The average was only 93 lb. of coal per person for one year, for everything during the entire winter, but the handicapped, elderly, sick, and young children were given more.

Transporting coal is dirty work, without machinery or mechanical aids (top). Coal sacks wore out very quickly, and were supplemented by army or air forces duffel bags (bottom). (U.S.A.F.)

Things Could Have Been Worse

The Essential Rations
As outlined on page 70, Berliners were tightly rationed. On the other hand, the food supply, while austere, was reasonably well balanced, with the emphasis on good nourishment. Milk came in in dried powder form, and potatoes, for example, were packed in dehydrated form. Disease and mortality rates actually improved in Berlin during the Airlift.

The British Ministry of Health advised on the choice of foods and their packaging style, drawing, no doubt, on personal experience. The British were still rationed in 1948, and housewives there still had to improvise and make do with some processed food.

Soak in Warm Water
Fortunately, in times of stress, relief is often found in a sense of humor. The caption to this cartoon from Der Insulaner was "The Dehydrated Baby—Soak for 20 minutes in warm water."

Radio
The only radio station within Berlin was located in the Communist sector and so the Americans built and operated RIAS (Radio in American Sector) beginning in September 1946. William F. Heimlich, the first director, was a former program supervisor for Radio Station WOSU, in Columbus, Ohio. By July 1947, the station was equipped with a 20 kw transmitter which broadcast several hours a day. When the blockade began, this increased to 24 hours a day, with new installations located in Schöneberg, opened on 6 July 1948. RIAS, known as the "Voice behind the Curtain," was heard all over Germany, when a new 100 kw transmitter was completed on 15 June 1949. Portable vans with loudspeakers often stood in the large public areas. RIAS Stations were added later in Hamburg, Munich, and Frankfurt.

> Radio showmaster Curt Flatow satirized: "To ensure that every Berliner has a warm room at Christmas, the date was being shifted to 24 July. Nor would decorations present a problem. The Allies were flying in powdered Christmas trees, easily reconstituted with water."

The Show Goes On
The Berlin Philharmonic Orchestra often played on RIAS, and there were theater productions. Sporting competitions continued, such as boxing, tennis, soccer, and horse racing, although athletes from the Soviet sector came in ever-decreasing numbers.

Movie theaters were hard hit—limited power supplies usually meant only one showing. But Berliners enjoyed the latest American films. Newsreel footage presented the Airlift to the rest of the world, countering Communist propaganda.

The Press
The Allies kept all ten local Berlin newspapers operating, even during the blockade, although most of them were reduced to two sheets of paper or four pages. The newsprint was cut into 500 lb. rolls, to fit into aircraft. 210 tons were delivered daily; later, an additional 60 tons a week were delivered for book and magazine productions. When the Soviets no longer allowed west Berlin newspapers to be sold in their sector, several of the large newspapers, which once printed 3 million copies daily, now only printed several hundred thousand. The blockade would have ruined these newspapers and only the Communist-supported paper would have survived. The used newsprint also provided an easy means of starting a fire in stoves.

Children's Airlift
Some of the happier moments of relief from the drudgery of living in Berlin during the Blockade were those occasions when some of the children were taken to western Germany for a respite. The excitement of riding in a big airplane was followed by a vacation, the joys of which are picturesquely described in the panel on page 70.

Other Sides of the Coin

Soviet Harrassment

Throughout the Airlift, the Soviets and Germans in the Eastern Zone harassed the Allies in almost any manner possible. Pilots would be blinded at night by searchlights and radios were jammed. Balloons were launched to obstruct takeoffs. Aircraft were hit 55 times by ground fire. Buzzing by Soviet aircraft made most pilots uneasy. Many of the old-time Airlifters had been wartime bomber pilots, conditioned to hold formation, even if 20 Russian Yaks were hassling. The Soviets hoped that new pilots would be bullied away from the corridors.

On 5 April 1948, just before the blockade began, a Vickers Viking of British European Airways, on a scheduled flight to Berlin, was buzzed by a Yak-3 fighter and then collided head-on. Pilots of both aircraft and 10 passengers in the Viking were killed.

The total number of harassment incidents can only be estimated, as the R.A.F. did not keep such records; but between August 1948 and 1949, US pilots reported 733 incidents as follows:

Incidents	Aug	Sep	Oct	Nov	Dec	Jan	Feb	Mar	Apr	May	Jun	Jul	Aug	Total
Buzzing	2	5	1	3	4	5	2	26	12	5	7	4	1	77
Close Flying	1	1	1	0	0	5	1	25	10	1	21	24	6	96
Flak	0	0	0	3	2	6	3	14	4	6	9	5	2	54
Air to Air Fire	0	0	0	1	0	0	2	5	3	0	0	3	0	14
Flares	0	0	0	1	2	7	8	14	2	9	5	7	4	59
Radio Interference	0	0	0	2	18	35	8	7	2	2	1	7	0	82
Searchlights	0	0	0	3	7	10	20	25	20	5	5	6	2	103
Air-Ground Fire	0	0	0	0	0	1	2	6	8	4	3	15	3	42
Ground Fire	0	0	0	3	4	5	5	10	4	6	8	9	1	55
Grd.Explosions	0	0	0	0	1	7	5	5	4	5	2	9	1	39
Rockets	0	0	0	0	0	3	0	0	0	0	1	0	0	4
Balloons	0	0	0	0	0	1	5	3	0	0	2	0	0	11
Chemical Laying	0	0	0	0	0	1	0	33	20	0	0	0	0	54
Bombing	0	0	0	0	0	0	3	3	1	2	25	2	0	36
Unident. Objects	0	0	0	1	0	0	2	0	0	1	3	0	0	7
Total	3	6	2	17	38	84	59	146	75	78	86	117	22	733

Pilots often worried about sabotage, especially after a series of crashes. 80 saboteurs were rumored to have infiltrated Tempelhof and Gatow Air Bases. Only one incident was actually reported, when Lt. Thomas Dab from Wiesbaden A.B., noted that the silk of his parachute had been replaced with GI blankets, and other parachutes in the 60th Troop Carrier Group were similarly tampered with. This frayed the nerves, but sabotage never became an issue.

Counter-Blockade

When the Soviets established the Blockade against Berlin, the Allies immediately began a counter blockade of all strategic materials (which included just about everything). The Soviet Zone had imported 320,000 tons of steel, 400,000 tons of chemical products and 110,000 automobile tires each year, for example. Only when the Soviets discovered that chrome, rubber, and other products could not be obtained elsewhere, did they begin to realize their predicament.

The success of the Berlin Airlift in maintaining ever-increasing tonnage figures and the unbroken spirit of the Berlin population, forced the Russians to realize their futility of the situation. Only a political solution could break the deadlock.

Total Blockade?

However we assess the Berlin Airlift and its achievements, the effectiveness of the Soviet blockade must also come into question. In 1949, the Berlin Wall had not yet been erected, so border crossings were not well protected. Travelling was restricted, but not impossible. The Soviets blocked only the main means of transportation, such as river, rail, and major road traffic between western Germany and the western sector of Berlin. Berlin was still a single city and the exchange of goods and services was impossible to totally disrupt overnight. The eastern sector of Berlin had more farms, while the western sector of Berlin manufactured many products that the East badly needed. Families from western Berlin would visit relatives in the eastern Zone, or vice versa, and even if on a small and informal scale, an exchange of goods occurred. This procedure was disapproved of by both sides and some controls were undertaken to prevent it.

Even during the blockade, there was a mutual exchange of goods between east and west. At Gatow, the Soviets could easily have turned off the electric power to the R.A.F.. On the other side, the British sector provided electric power to a Russian fighter station. Several such convenient arrangements existed. Generally speaking, the Russians turned off the power to the city of Berlin. The blockade was more psychological than physical.

The United States also enforced a number of counter-blockade measures, as a show of force. Economic sanctions were placed upon the Soviet Union. The Panama Canal was closed to ships serving the Soviet Union. A boycott of eastern newspapers led to an end of the Communist press in western Berlin. The formal export of goods from the western sector of Berlin to the East was prohibited. This polarized both sides, with the Eastern Zone of Germany turning more and more to Russia for economic support while the Western Zone of Germany and western Berlin were supplied by the United States and its allies.

French Contribution

Preoccupied as they were with the conflict in French Indo-China, the French were unable to contribute directly to the airborne action of the Airlift. However, some French aircraft were to be seen flying in the corridors—Junkers-Ju 52/3m's and Douglas Dakotas—en route to the French Zone of Berlin, delivering supplies to the French garrison there.

> General Jean Ganeval, the French commandant in Berlin, quickly agreed, on 25 August 1948, to the construction of Tegel in the French sector. Built by U.S. Berlin Military Post Engineers, the runway was soon completed. The French supplied all ground installations and provided the loading and unloading of aircraft. Operations began on 5 November 1948, and the runway opened to civilian aircraft on 15 January 1949.
>
> Unfortunately, a 200-foot high radio tower was located dangerously near the approach path to Tegel. It stood at the edge within the French sector, but belonged to a Communist controlled radio station. Two requests to remove the tower were denied by the Soviets.
>
> General Tunner recalled: "...General Ganeval invited the detachment which we had stationed there (Tegel), composed of some 20 officers and men, to come up to his office for a mysterious meeting. When all had arrived, General Ganeval shut and locked the door. The procedure seemed somewhat strange at first, but the General provided such excellent refreshments and exuded such Gallic charm, that all suspicions were allayed. Suddenly, in the midst of the merriment, a mighty blast rattled the window panes and shook the room. French and Americans alike dashed to the window just in time to see the huge radio tower slowly topple to the ground. "You will have no more trouble with the tower," said the General softly. The Soviets protested and attempted to blame the Americans. But the French had also provided an alibi. The Americans had been locked in.

The Airlift Ends

Negotiations
In February 1949, American and Soviet delegates began negotiations to end the Blockade. The Soviets realized that they had failed to break western determination and further efforts would be counter-productive. On 4 May 1949, a Four-Power Communique announced that the blockade would end one minute after midnight on 12 May. Ten British vehicles made the first truck convoy from Helmstedt to Berlin. At 6:30 a.m. the first train from West Germany arrived in Berlin. The Mayor, Ernst Reuter, along with the head of the German Government, Dr. Konrad Adenauer, publicly expressed their appreciation to the military governments and their respective nations, and to the men and women who had made the Berlin Airlift a success. In the City Assembly at Schöneberg a special meeting was called not only to mark the occasion, but to bid farewell to General Clay, who was returning to the United States after being stationed in Germany for four years. He received a standing ovation.

Gen. Frank Howley, Commandant of the American sector of Berlin, stated his feelings about the Airlift in his book, *Berlin Command*: "It is conceivable that the Russians credited us with the ability to bring in food for the city. We had been doing it for months, but what they didn't count on was coal. Who ever heard of supplying a city with coal by air?"

Although the Soviet blockade officially ended on 12 May 1949, the Airlift continued to restock supplies in the city, in case the Soviets intended to block access again. A German rail strike a few days later made Airlift operations essential, with rail service not resuming until July. Operationally, such a huge undertaking could not be terminated suddenly. The relocation of personnel and equipment would have to be spread over a period of time.

Last U.S. Flights
U.S.A.F.E. operations ended at Celle A.B., when the 317th Troop Carrier Wing ceased operations on 1 August 1949. By 1 September, the 60th Troop Carrier Wing wound up at Fassberg A.B.. The final Operation Vittles flight left Rhein-Main A.B. on 30 September 1949, and was commemorated by a formation of aircraft flying overhead. One of the aircraft was painted: "Last Vittles Flight, 1,783,572.7 Tons to Berlin." Capt. Perry Immel, commander of the flight, had flown 403 missions. The crew were long-time airlift veterans: 1st.Lt. Charles M. Reece (325 missions), 1st.Lt. James C. Powell (180 missions) and TSgt. Matthew M. Terrenzi (more than 40 missions).

General Cannon transferred personnel back to their duty stations in five phases over a period of 180 days. The Combined Airlift Task Force was deactivated on 1 September 1949. General Tunner resumed his duties as MATS Deputy Commander for Operations. By 31 October the phase-out was complete.

R.A.F. Withdraws
R.A.F. contracts with the civilian carriers expired between 10 and 15 August, 1949. 206 Squadron redeployed to Lyneham and 47 Squadron returned to Topcliffe, effective on 15 August. On 22 August, 59 Squadron returned to Bassingbourn; on 29 August, 18 Squadron flew to Waterbeach and ten Yorks of 511 Squadron returned to Lyneham. By 1 September 1949, R.A.F. personnel on temporary duty assignment were back home in England. The final R.A.F. Airlift flights were on 6 September 1949, 30 Squadron returned to Abingdon on 12 September, and 10 Squadron returned to Oakington on 26 September. On 14 October 1949, Headquarters Group 46 at Lüneberg closed down.

Airfields were closed down as follows:

Airfield	Last Airlift Flight	Airfield	Last Airlift Flight
Celle	1200 July 31, 1949	Fassberg	0600 August 27, 1949
Fuhlsbüttel	2400 August 15, 1949	Lübeck	2000 September 23, 1949
Rhein-Main	1845 September 30, 1949	Schleswigland	October 6, 1949
Wiesbaden	0800 September 2, 1949	Wunstorf	2000 August 29, 1949

Celebration
On 13 May 1949, 300,000 Berliners celebrated in front of City Hall at Schöneberg to mark the end of the blockade. Ernst Reuter said in his speech:

> The attempt to bring us to our knees has failed. It failed because our call to the world was heard and answered.

Gen. Clay then spoke:

> The attempt to blockade Berlin was a challenge to all free peoples... Without the Berliners the Airlift could have never succeeded. They were dependent upon the Airlift and suffered difficult economic hardships and a long winter in unheated homes. Still, the Berliners and their leaders never wavered in their determination for freedom.
>
> Berlin can be proud of its part in this victory. They discovered their own potential. We can be sure that Berlin will never give up its freedom, rather it will lead the way for all of Germany in the principle of peace.

Medals and Decorations
U.S. Air Force personnel involved with the Berlin Airlift received, as authorized by Congress, **The Medal for Humane Action**, to recognize their meritorious participation in the Airlift. The colors of the ribbon represent the Coat of Arms of Berlin, white and black, against a blue background, symbolizing the sky.

The **Berlin Airlift Clasp** was authorized by the Chiefs of Staff of the Army and the Air Force, and was later also approved by the Navy. It was a gold-colored miniature C-54 aircraft used in Operations Vittles, worn on the service ribbon of the Army, Navy, or Air Force Occupation Service Medal, with the nose pointing upward at a 30-degree angle toward the wearer's right. Military personnel who served 90 consecutive days or more, on their permanent or temporary duty in support of the Airlift, were authorized to receive the clasp.

A number of soldiers earned other medals during the Airlift; 1 Distinguished Flying Cross, 2 Air Service Medals, 68 Legion of Merit, 1 Cheney Award, and 246 Commendations. Seven awards were given to civilians for meritorious services.

Reflections

Organization
The German defeat and loss of Stalingrad during the Second World War was caused by the failure of the Luftwaffe to establish an adequate airlift. 400 to 500 aircraft, mostly Junkers Ju-52/3m's, poured into the operation, many not winterized. German mechanics were over-burdened, resulting in the loss of 300 aircraft. The Luftwaffe transported only 90 tons of supplies daily to the encircled German troops in Stalingrad, whereas 300 tons were required. These amounted to only a fraction of that necessary for Berlin. The Soviets, therefore, apparently felt secure in assuming Berlin was too large to supply by air.

The Berlin Airlift demonstrated a united Allied resolve against Soviet expansion and the Cold War. The Soviets were mightily impressed by the effective use of this air transport capacity, and could not have accomplished such an airlift themselves in 1948/49.

Weather
The clement weather played an important factor in the success. The average temperature during the worst winter days was uncharacteristically much the same as during the average autumn or early spring. Flights were halted only twice because of bad weather.

Heavy Lifters
The U.S. Air Force realized that the future of its air transport needs depended upon large, economical and reliable aircraft. Size was the dominating factor, not speed. The apparent necessity for such large transport planes became obvious, resulting in the Douglas C-124 Globemaster II (replacing the C-74 Globemaster I). This aircraft could carry 25 tons and arrived during the final days of the Berlin airlift. The C-124 has since been replaced by several newer aircraft. The Lockheed C-5A Galaxy is the largest transport aircraft operated by the U.S.A.F. today. Seventeen C-5A flights into Berlin could match an entire day's worth of C-54 flights.

Many years after the Berlin Airlift, the Soviet Union developed several large transport aircraft. The Antonov An-124 can carry 150 tons, while its cousin, the An-225, with a gross weight of 600 tons, can carry 250 tons, a load that is not far short of the maximum gross weight of a DC-10.

The Berlin Airlift in Perspective
Today's aircraft are much larger but no airlift has matched the volume of material transported during the Berlin Airlift. **Operation Provide Promise**, which provided food and supplies to war-torn Yugoslavia, became the longest, single humanitarian airlift in U.S. history, transporting 160,000 tons in 45 months, but the combined tonnage did not reach a tenth of that provided during the Berlin Airlift. More tonnage was transported in a single month of the Berlin Airlift, than during the entire Operation Provide Promise.

Warehousing
One lesson learned was the necessity for capacity on the ground as well as in the air. The U.S.A.F. experienced great difficulties providing storage near their airfields. As a result, food was not immediately available for Airlift. Twenty-four hours were required to move food from warehouses, to the railhead or to the airfield. The R.A.F. on the other hand, had ample storage space at both Wunstorf and Celle.

Growth
The U.S.A.F. transport command has grown and changed since Berlin. From its humble beginnings as the **Air Corps Ferrying Command** (29 May 1941–19 June 1942), it quickly grew to become the **Air Transport Command (ATC)** (20 June 1942–31 May 1948 (Army Air Force)). The **Military Air Transport Service (MATS)**, was created with the development of the U.S. Air Force (1 June 1948–31 December 1965) and expanded into the well-known **Military Airlift Command (MAC)** (1 January 1966–31 March 1992) which supported the Vietnam conflict and many other military and humanitarian operations. The political changes that have occurred since the fall of the Berlin wall have led to a major restructuring of the U.S. Air Force. The **Air Mobility Command (AMC)** was created on 1 April 1992, to meet this new situation and prepare the Air Force for its role into the year 2000.

Diplomatic Weapon
As stated in the *Air Force* magazine, September 1948: "For the first time in history, the United States is employing its Air Force as a diplomatic weapon." Since then air transport has often served as a flexible tool for executing U.S. national policy. Humanitarian airlifts have assisted nations around the world when in need, from the effects of natural disaster, war, or disease. Since the Berlin Airlift, Rhein-Main A.B. alone has been directly involved or has supported some 170 humanitarian airlifts of the U.S. Air Force to locations throughout Europe, Asia, and Africa.

The Berlin Airlift also provided valuable experience in air traffic control methods, in operation techniques, and aircraft maintenance. This experience was not only beneficial for future military operations but also assisted the development of civilian aviation. In June 1950, the **Korean War** began. MATS would transport 80,000 tons of supplies and 214,000 troops, again only a fraction of the tonnage delivered to Berlin. Once more, **General William H. Tunner** was placed in command. Tunner died on 19 June 1983, and is buried in Arlington National Cemetery, Sec. 3. Lot 4072 B.

Aftermath
After the Berlin Airlift, the new State, the **Federal Republic of Germany**, was formed with a constitution written by 23 May 1949, and its first elections held on 14 August. The American Military Occupational control over the German population was turned over to the U.S. State Department on 21 September 1949, thereby allowing the creation of the new German state that same day.

The Soviet blockade of Berlin led to the unified efforts of England, France, and the United States during the Airlift, and to the creation of the **North Atlantic Treaty Organization (NATO)** which was created shortly before the end of the blockade. On 4 April 1949, twelve nations signed the NATO treaty in Washington D.C., to being a new era of peace in Europe. The Federal Republic of Germany joined the organization on 9 May 1955, which led to the Soviet formation of the **Warsaw Pact** on 14 May. The creation of the **German Democratic Republic** (East Germany) occurred in October 1949. During the following years numerous bases and military installations were built in many parts of Europe, especially in Germany, France, Spain, and England. Europe experienced a massive build-up of military personnel and equipment as part of the development of NATO. In the long run, this unified determination managed to bring down the political wall dividing two German nations, a wall that was, in Berlin, solid brick, stone, and concrete. The Berlin Airlift, it could be said, was the first step towards the eventual decline and ultimate end to the Cold War.

Memorials

Berlin's Gratitude
The Luftbrücke Dank, the **Airlift Gratitude Foundation**, was created ten years after the airlift ended by Willy Brandt, then Mayor of Berlin. The charter reads:

"In memory of the sacrifices made by the American, English, French and German people during the Berlin blockade, through the establishment of the Airlift in the period from 28 June 1948 to 30 September 1949, a foundation is to be created by the City of Berlin from funds contributed in gratitude for the Airlift.... Its goal is to express the ties between Berlin and the Airlift nations." Donations were collected and the funds are still used to assist the children and families of those pilots and crew who lost their lives during the Airlift. Their address is: Stiftung Luftbrückedank, Berliner Rathaus, 10173 Berlin.

On 10 July 1951, the **Airlift Memorial** was dedicated to those who lost their lives during the Airlift. Although officially the design, by **Prof. Edward Ludwig**, had only won second place in the competition, this was the one actually used. It is located in the large circular park in front of the entrance to Tempelhof Airport in Berlin. The arch is 63 ft. high, and is formed by three sections, representing the three nations involved in the Airlift: America, Britain, and France. Along the base, the names of those killed are inscribed. On the occasion, General Clay gave a short but memorable speech:

"It is with sincere humbleness that I stand here today to participate in this inspiring memorial to my esteemed British and American Air crewmen and German workers whose lives were given so that the Berlin Airlift would not fail.

I remember personally the many thousands of Berliners, almost half of them women, who took the rubble from bombed out buildings, who took the very rocks and stones from the streets and built them up, layer by layer, into the runways at Tegel and Tempelhof and Gatow, so that we might have ample, safe landing space....

The men who died, did so in a worthy cause and this lasting memorial to them should serve as a reminder to all the world that free men are willing to lay down their lives for the principles in which they believe.

Es ist wunderbar wieder bei Euch in Berlin zu sein. Auf Wiedersehen."

Other Memorials
In May 1985 a copy of the Berlin memorial was erected at **Rhein-Main A.B.** to commemorate the major role that this base played during the Airlift. The memorial is flanked by a C-47 and a C-54 aircraft. A third smaller copy of the memorial was dedicated at **Celle** on 24 June 1988. A fourth and smallest copy stands at **Scott A.F.B** in Illinois. It is part of the Airlift/Tanker Hall of Fame Memorial and was dedicated on 29 May 1991, as part of the Military Airlift Command's fiftieth anniversary. A bronze bust of Gen. William H. Tunner stands nearby. His was the first individual bust to be unveiled in 1989, as part of the Hall of Fame Walkway. This entire project is sponsored by the General Robert E. Huyser Chapter of the Airlift Association.

A memorial window was donated in 1951, to the newly completed base chapel, by the **Rhein-Main Airmen's Club** in memory of the those Rhein-Main airmen who were killed. The window was designed by the Offenbach artist **Karl Lutz** and crafted by glassmaster **H. Wiessenrieder,** and made from 1,500 individual pieces of glass. The Latin inscription "Vita Nostra Fratribus Laborantibus" translates "Our lives for brothers in distress." A figure to the left represents the American people, while two figures to the right symbolize a mother and child of Berlin.

The Air Force named the streets of the **Lindsey Air Station** near Wiesbaden A.B. housing area in honor of those who died. C.W.O. Lloyd A. Taliaferro, Installation Engineer, gave several streets on Rhein-Main A.B. their names, in memory of those from the base who had lost their lives during the Airlift.

Aircraft Preserved
Three former airlift aircraft were located in Berlin: a C-54 Skymaster at **Tempelhof**, a Hastings at **Gatow**, and a C-47 (which once stood in Gatow) in the **Technical Museum, Berlin.** The Tempelhof Skymaster has now been moved, for safe keeping, to the Technical Museum.

Prof. Edward Ludwig's symbolic design stands impressively in the forecourt at the entrance to Tempelhof Airport in Berlin. (George Wegemann)

The Spirit of Freedom

Organizations dedicated to the Berlin Airlift:

Luftbrücke Chapter of the Airlift Tanker Association e.V., Rhein-Main A.B., Bldg. 347, 60549 Frankfurt / Main, Germany. Tel. 01149 69 699 7179.

Formed by a group of American Air Force officers and Germans on Rhein-Main A.B. on 18 June 1984, this organization was instrumental in raising funds and erecting of the memorial located on base, and obtaining the two aircraft located there.

Berlin Airlift Veterans Association (BAVA), Bill Gross, 7616 Upper Sequin Road, Converse, Texas 78109, USA.

The BAVA was created by veterans of the Berlin Airlift, in 1990, with Col. Kenneth Herman as it's president. It is the largest organization dedicated to the memory of this event. Membership is open to the general public.

The **British Berlin Airlift Association** represents the members and involvement of Operation Plainfare. The Secretary is Sqn. Ldr. Frank Stillwell, 9 Barnards Hill, Marlow, Bucks, SL 7 2 NX, England.

South African Air Force Berlin Airlift Reunion Committee holds an annual reunion in October. The chairman is Maj.Gen. D.M. Ralston, P.O. Box 12251, Clubview 0014, South Africa.

Museums of the Berlin Airlift:

Rhein-Main A.B. Historical Exhibit, 469th ABG / PA, Unit 7420 Box 130, APO AE 09050, USA or Kelkheimer Str. 29A, 65779 Kelkheim, Germany Tel./ FAX 01149 6195 61350.

This museum actively collects historical items related to the Berlin Airlift and U.S. forces stationed in Germany and now offers one of the largest collections. It was founded by Roger Seeholzer, Hector Cebazas and John Provan in 1993.

Fassberg Luftbrücke Museum, Herr Rainer Kruppik, S 1 Info, Postfach 916 / 1, 29324 Fassberg. (Open from 1 April to 30 September, Sundays 14:00 - 16:00)

Two Quonset huts and a railway car provide display space for artifacts to provide authentic atmosphere of conditions during the Airlift.

Displays or collections of Berlin Airlift memorabilia are also included in several museums:

- **U.S.A.F. Museum,** Wright-Patterson A.F.B., Ohio, USA.
- **Travis A.F.B.,** Ca., USA.
- **Air Mobility Command**, Scott A.F.B., Ill., USA.

Pictures courtesy Berlin Aircraft Historical Foundation.

Berlin Aircraft Historical Foundation

Located at the Robert J. Miller Airpark, PO Box 782, Farmingdale, NJ 07727, USA, this organization is dedicated to preserving the memory of the Berlin Airlift in a most effective form—by maintaining the airworthiness of aircraft that are representative of the actual fleets used in 1948–49, and by making demonstration flights at airshows.

Of special pride is a Douglas C-54E (see page 23) that was one of the 330 Skymasters that were called back into active service for the Airlift. Named *The Spirit of Freedom*, it will recreate this unshrinking characteristic on the feats of the Candy Bomber (see page 63). It serves as a flying museum, with photographic panels lining the cabin, and as both a memorial and a classroom; and it was on hand for Berlin's celebration of the 50th Anniversary.

Still flying today, this Douglas R5D served in the Berlin Airlift from 26 June 1948 to 12 May 1949.

Not content with the historic Skymaster, the B.A.H.F. has acquired, in Feb 1997, a Boeing C-97G (see page 28). Named Deliverance*, it will join the C-54E in preserving the memory of the Berlin Airlift.*

The Final Count

The Start
The Soviet Blockade began on 24 June 1948. The first Airlift flight was by a British Royal Air Force Douglas C-47 Dakota on 25 June. Next day, the United States Air Force delivered 80 tons to begin **Operation Vittles**, while the British named their effort **Operation Plainfare**.

The Momentum
By the next month, the combined fleets were hauling up to 1,000 tons per day, and, as the larger Douglas C-54s began to arrive in large numbers from as far away as the western Pacific, the daily tonnage, most of it coal, grew to more than 5,000 tons a day.

Steadily increasing the tempo, the Airlift reached its peak on Sunday, 16 April 1949, when the "Easter Parade" achieved a record of 1,398 flights, at almost one flight for every minute of a 24-hour period, and delivered 12,849 tons of goods into Berlin in one day.

The Aircraft
The U.S. Air Force used 330 Douglas C54s (21 of them were Navy R5Ds), 105 Douglas C-47s, 5 Fairchild C-82s, one Douglas C-74 Globemaster, and one Boeing C-97A (see pages 23–29). The British R.A.F. used 40 C-47 Dakotas, 35 Avro Yorks, and 26 Handley Page Hastings; and these were supplemented by a motley assortment of aircraft chartered from non-scheduled airlines (see pages 48–57). The U.S. non-scheds also contributed (see page 45).

The Loads
The Americans carried the majority of the tonnage, most of it coal, but also the flour for the bread, and dehydrated potatoes, and other foods. The British carried the liquid fuel—oil, gasoline, kerosene, and diesel—plus the salt and the fish. The statistics are on the page opposite.

The People
Figures as to the number of personnel involved in the Berlin Airlift can only be estimated. The *New Yorker* magazine stated that 75,000 people were involved, 45,000 German cargo loaders and workers, 12,000 U.S.A.F. personnel, 8,000 R.A.F. personnel (including Australians, new Zealanders, and South Africans); 3,000 displaced persons from the Baltic states, 800 U.S. Naval, and 2,000 U.S. Army Airlift Support personnel. These figures do not include American, British and French civilians employed in military government agencies, or contract airlines.

Breaking the back of the Blockade. When, at Easter, the U.S.A.F. brought in almost 13,000 tons in one day, all doubts were cast aside.

The U.S. Navy, and some German workers, celebrate the end of the Blockade in no uncertain terms. (U.S.A.F. pictures)

Into the Book of Records

TONNAGES

Commodity	U.S.	British
Coal	1,421,730	164,800
Food	296,303	241,713
Military Supplies		18,239
Liquid Fuel	65,540	92,282
Miscellaneous		25,202
TOTALS	**1,783,573**	**542,236**
	2,325,809	

The determination to succeed was evident right from the start. The C-47s which started the airlift worked right around the clock—and so did the airmen and the troops. (U.S.A.F.)

The C-54 Skymasters could not operate without solid concrete or P.S.P. runways, and a crash program of construction early in the Airlift was one of the keys to ultimate success. (U.S.A.F.)

Bibliography

13th Anniversary 862nd Engineer Aviation Battalion, by Lt.Col. Carl G. Anderson; no pub., 1956.

The TC in the Vittles Operation, in Army Transportation Journal, Nov.–Dec. 1948, P. 10.

Aviation Operations: "A Special Study of Operation Vittles," Conover-Mast Publications, New York, April 1949.

Berlin Airlift, an Account of the British Contribution by Dudley Barker; H.M.S.O., London, 1949

Blockade, Airlift and Airlift Gratitude Foundation, Concerning the History of the Berlin Crisis 1948-49, by Jack O. Bennett; no date or publisher given.

Bastion Berlin, by Lowell Bennett; Friedrich Rudl Verleger Union, 1952.

Erinnerungsstätte Luftbrücke, Fassberg 1948–49, by Oberleut. Böltzig; Fassberg, 1990.

Bridge Across the Sky, by Richard Collier; McGraw-Hill, New York, 1978.

The Berlin Airlift, by Paul Fisher; United Aircraft Corporation, *Beehive*, 1949

Airbridge to Berlin, by D.M. Giangreco; Topeka, Kansas, 1988.

The Candy Bomber, by Gail S. Halvorsen; Horizon Publishers, Utah, 1990.

Berlin Command by Gen. Frank Howley; Cornwall Press, N.Y., 1950.

The Berlin Airlift, by Robert Jackson; Patrick Stephens, Northamptonshire, 1988.

A Reporter in Germany, by E.J. Kahn; in the New Yorker, May 14, 1949.

MAC and the Legacy of the Berlin Airlift, by Roger D. Launius; Scott AFB, Ill. 1989.

The Berlin Air Lift, by Elisabeth S. Lay; (HS 169) Part I: 21 June–31 December 1948, Part II: 1 January–30 September 1949, Historical Division, European Command, Karlsruhe, 1952. (declassified in 1964)

Mr. Marseille, by Charles L. Lunsford; in Flying Safety, pages 2–5, 1995.

The Berlin Airlift, by P.L. MacGregor; in the South African Air Force Journal, July 1949, Vol. 1, No. 3, P. 41–46.

Medical History of the Berlin Airlift, by Lt.Col. Harry G. Moseley; in U.S. Armed Forced Medical Journal, November 1950, Vol. 1, No. 11, P. 1249–1263.

Airlift to Berlin, in National Geographic Magazine; (no author), May 1949, P. 595–614.

Medical Aspects of Operation Vittles, by Lt. R.D. Nauman; in Journal of Aviation Medicine, Vol. 22, Feb. 1951.

Berlin-Blockade und Luftbrücke 1948/49, Analyse und Dokumentation, by Uwe Prell and Lothar Wilder; Berlin Verlag, 1987.

Rhein-Main A.B. Public Affairs: "The Gateway," 1948–1949. (Weekly Base newspaper)

Pure Religion, the story of Church Welfare since 1930, by Glen Rudd; Utah, P. 245–261, 1995.

The United States and the Berlin Blockade, 1948–1949, a Study in Crisis Decision-making, by Avi Shlaim; University of California, 1983.

United States Air Forces in Europe—Historical Highlights 1942–1992, by Dr. Thomas Snyder; HQ USAFE, Ramstein Air Base, Germany, P.1–40, 1993.

Das American Friends Service Committee und die Humanitäre Hilfe, by James F. Tent; Weserdruckerei, Stolzenau, 1996.

The Berlin Airlift, Mission Accomplished, in Troop Information Program Service: TIPS, May 1949, Vol. 6, No. 27, Tokyo, Japan.

Over the Hump by Gen. William H. Tunner; USAF Warrior Studies, Office of Air Force History, Washington D.C. 0-474-054, 340 pages, 1985.

A Report on Operation Plainfare, by Air Marshal T.M. Williams; British Air Ministry, Bielefeld, April 1950.

Thirty Years On, The Berlin Airlift- A Reassessment, by P.R. Wood; in the Royal Air Force Quarterly, Vol. 18, No. 3, P. 226–238.

Berlin Airlift, USAFE, Headquarters: 26 June 1948–30 September 1949, Restricted Report from 1949. (US Navy Archives, Naval Ship Yards, Washington D.C.)

Airlift, a History of Military Air Transport, by David Wragg; Airlife Publishing Ltd., P. 70–82, 1986.

Index

Accidents, complete record, 66-67
Adenauer, Dr. Konrad, expresses appreciation, 74
A.F.N.-Armed Force Network, 64
A.F.S.C. (Quakers), relief work, 60
Air Contractors, Dakota, 55P; Fleet, 57T
Air Corps Ferrying Command, lifespan dates, 75
Air Corridors, 22M, 32M, 33M, 58
Air Force, U.S., created 1947, 13
Air Mobility Command (AMC)
  Lifespan dates, 75
  Museum, 77
Air Transport Command (A.T.C.)
  Merges with NATS, 46
  Lifespan dates, 75
Air Transport (C.I.) Fleet list, 57T
Aircraft Engineering & Maintenance Co., 40
Airflight, 37; aircraft, 50P, 52P, 57T
Airlift Laffs, Schuffert cartoons, 65
Airwork, Fleet list, 57T
Alaskan Air Command, supplies aircraft, 30T
Alaskan Airlines, 45
Allierte Militärberhörde Geld, 13
Allied Occupation Currency, 13
American Overseas Airlines, (A.O.A.)
  Participates in Airlift, 44; **Machat C-54**, 44
  Load carrying record, 44P; CARE shipments, 60
Antonov An-124, load capability compared, 75
Arnold, Gen. H.H. 'Hap,' inspects Marston Mat, 43
Aquila Airways
  Carries salt, 54; Fleet list, 57T
Australian Air Force, Royal, 31, 38
Austria, independence, 10
Avro Anson, early R.A.F. operation, 18
Avro Lancaster/Lancastrian
  Machat, Specifications, 52, 52P
  Carries liquid fuel, 31; Flight Refuelling, 31P
  British fleets, 57T; Fatal crash, 67T
Avro Lincoln, British independent airline fleets, 57T
Avro 688 Tudor
  Machat, specifications Tudor 5, 50
  B.S.A.A. Tudor 1, 50P; Airflight Tudor 2, 50P
  Fleet Record, 51T
  British independent airline fleets, 57T
  Fatal crash, 67T
Avro 685 York
  Machat, specifications, 51
  R.A.F. fleet, 16, 21, 51P, 56P
  Special flight, 51P; **Fleet Record, 51T**
  Skyways fleet, 57T; Fatal crashes, 67T

Bachus, 1st. Lt. Harry, pin-points candy drop, 63
Bamberg Harold, heads Eagle Aviation, 48
Bank Deutscher Länder, 13
Barkley, Vice President Alven, visits troops, 64
BEALCOM, 21
Bennett, Connie, *Over 21* show, 64
Bergen, Edgar, entertains troops, 64
Berlin
  Isolation, 15, 15M, 15P; Rationing, 70, 72; Bread baking, 70; Trees, 71; Power supply, 71
  Civilian employment in Airlift, 71
  Industrial production maintained, 71
  R.I.A.S. radio station, newspapers, 72
  Children's Airlift, 72
Berlin Aircraft Historical Foundation, 77
Berlin Airlift Clasp authorized, 74
Berlin Airlift Co-ordination Committee, 17
Berlin, Irving, entertains troops, 64
Berlin Philharmonic Orchestra, plays for Berlin radio station, 72
B.H.A.C. (Berliner Hilfswerke), relief work, 60
Big Lift, movie film, 64
Bipartite Control Office (BECO), 21
Bird Dog, Operation, 13
Black Market, 12, 12P
Black Friday, confusion at Tempelhof, 20
Blockade
  Begins, 15, 78; Counter-blockade, 73
  Discussion of effectiveness, 73
Boeing B-17 Flying Fortress, drafted into action, 44
Boeing B-29 Superfortress, deterrent, 15
Boeing C-97 Stratofreighter
  Operation at end of Airlift, 21, 28
  Machat, Specifications, 28, 28P
  Aircraft preserved by BAHF, 77P
Bohemia, German protectorate, 10
Bond Air Services, At Fuhlsbüttel, 38
  Halifax aircraft, **Machat, 49**, 49P
  Fleet list, 57T
Booth, Col., commander, Tempelhof A.B., 34
Bowman, Sgt. Perry A., surprise assignment, 16
Brandt, Willy, Mayor of Berlin, creates Airlift Gratitude Foundation, 76
Bristol 170 Freighter
  Machat, specifications, 56
  Silver City Airways, 57P
  British independent airline fleets, 57T
British American Air Services (B.A.A.S.), British charter company
  At Schleswigland, 38; Halifax aircraft, 48P
  Fleet list, 57T
British Berlin Airlift Association, 77
British European Airways (B.E.A.)
  Directs British private operators, 16, 56
British Nederland Air Services,
  Douglas Dakota, 55P
  Fleet list, 57T
British Overseas Airways Corp. Fleet list, 57T
B.S.A.A. (British South American Airways)
  Operates from Wunstorf, 37
  Tudor aircraft, **Machat, 50**, 50P, 52
  Fleet list, 57T
Bückeburg, base, British European Airways, 56
Burtonwood, British Air Base
  Reopened for Boeing B-29s, 15
  Reopened for Airlift C-54s, 39
  Maintenance from Oberpfaffenhofen, 40

Camel Caravan, special C-47, **Machat**, 64
Candy Bomber, the, 62-63 , 62P
Cannon, Lt. Gen. John K., Replaces LeMay, 30
CARE (Cooperative for American Remittances to Europe)
  Review of supply of packages, 60
Carnegie Illinois, develops Marston Mat, 43
Caritas, relief work, 60
Cartoons, 64-65, 72
Carver, Navy Lt. Margaret, first woman to serve in Airlift, 69
Cawthray, Reverend Donald, R.A.F. chaplain, 16
C.D.U. (Christian Democratic Union), 11
Celle, R.A.F. base, **37**, 37M; Runway construction, 42P; Memorial, 76
Children's Airlift, 72
Chocolate Pilot (Gail Halverson), 63
Christmas, children's parties, 58
Christmas Caravan, entertainment for troops, 64
Ciro's Aviation, British charter company
  Douglas Dakota, 55P
  Fleet list, 57T
Clarence, the Camel, shipped by C-47, **Machat**, 64
Clay, General Lucius D.
  U.S. Military Governor, 11, 14P
  Celebration speech, 74
  Dedicates Airlift Memorial, 76
Clay's Pigeons, 14
Coal shipments
  1,000,000th ton, 58; Unloading record, 59
  Pilot's comments to Gen. Tunner, 65
  Man-handling work, 71P; Statistics, 79
Combined Airlift Task Force, 17
  Standard Operating Procedures, 32M, 33M
Composite Airlift Task Force (C.A.L.T.F.), 30
Consolidated B-24 Liberator
  Machat, Specification, 53
  Scottish Airlines fleet, 57T
Continental Air Command, supplies aircraft, 30T
Control Zones, 11, 11M
Cordon Sanitaire, Soviet security policy, 9, 9M
Corridors, (see Air Corridors)
Currency Reform, 13, 13P
Czechoslovakia, annexed by Germany; regains independence, 10

Danzig, League of Nations Free Zone, 10
Deliverance, C-97 preserved by BHAF, 77P
Dorr, Col. Henry, Commander, Tempelhof A.B., 14
Douglas C-47 Skytrain, 14P
  Machat, specifications, 19, 64
  Fleet build-up, 21;Replaced by C-54, 30
  Maintenance, 40P, 41P
  Crash in Berlin city street, 67P; Fatal crashes, 66T
  Aircraft preserved in Berlin, 76
  Night-time operations, 79P
Douglas C-54 Skymaster
  Joins Airlift, 19, 19P
  Black Friday incident, 20
  Fleet build-up, 21, 21P, 23P; total numbers, 40
  Machats, 23, 24, 25; Dust Jacket Cover (USAF); 44 (A.O.A.); 45 (Seaboard, Transocean, Alaska)
  Specifications, 23, 44
  Replaces C-47, 30, 30P
  Located at Fassberg and Celle, 37, 37P
  Maintenance procedures, 40, 40P, 41P
  Line-up at Rhein-Main, 46P
  Operating procedures, 47 (chart)
  Fatal crashes, 66T
  Aircraft preserved at Tempelhof, 76
Douglas C-74 Globemaster I
  Machat, Specifications, 26, 26P
  Airlifts engines, 69
Douglas C-124, minor contribution, 75
Douglas Dakota (R.A.F. C-47)
  Early airlift operation and fleet, 16, 21, 21P, 38P
  Machat, Specifications, 18, 55
  Summary of civil Dakota tonnages, **55T**
  Air Contractors, Ciro's Aviation, British Nederland, Hornton Airways, Scottish Airlines, 55P
  British independent airline fleets, 57T
  Fatal crashes, 67T
Douglas DC-3 (see Douglas C-47 and Dakota)
  Production record, 19
Douglas DC-4 (see Douglas C-54 Skymaster)
Douglas R5D (Naval C-54)
  Machat, Specifications 29
  Maintenance at Moffett NAS and Lockheed, 40
  Fatal crash, 66T
  Preserved as flying museum, 77
  Spirit of Freedom, The, 77, 77P
Duffey, Peter, B.S.A.A. Pilot, assesses Avro Tudor performance, 50

Eagle Aviation, At Fuhlsbüttel, 38
  Machat Halifax, 48 and Dust Jacket Cover
  Fleet list, 57T
Eagles Club, services amenity, 36
Easter Parade, Record airlift tonnage , 59, 78, 78P
Erding, Air Force Depot, 39, 40
Eureka Radar Beacons, 32

Fairchild C-82 Packet
  Machat, Specifications, 27, 27P
  Delivers P.S.P., 43
Fassberg A.B.
  R.A.F. base, **37, 37M**
  Luftbrücke Museum, 77
Felgentreff, Kurt, tragic death, 71
Fernandez, Lt. Col. Manuel 'Pete,', 20
Ferrying Command, lifespan dates, 75
Finkenwerder, R.A.F. marine base in Elbe river, 39
Finlayson, Sqd. Ldr. P.J.S., first pilot into Schleswigland, 38
Fisher, Col. Dale D., base commander, Fassberg, 37
Flatow, Curt, shifts date of Christmas, 72
Flight Refuelling Ltd., British charter company
  Machat Lancaster, 51
  Liquid fuel carrier, 31, 31P
  Based at Fuhlsbüttel, 38
  Fleet list, 57T
Flour shipments, 70, 70P
Forman, Col. Red, on Tunner's staff, 20
Forward Airfield Supply Organization (FASO), 17
Foster, Mr. G.A.C.H., liaison between British charter companies and R.A.F.
French Air Force, At Tegel, 35; Indochina conflict, 73
Frohnau Beacon, 33, 58
Fuhlsbüttel, Hamburg Airport, **38**, 38M, 38P

Gallagher, Gen. Philip E., commands U.S. Army activities, 68
Ganevel, Gen. Jean, solves problem at Tegel, 73
Gatow, Airfield in British Zone of Berlin
  First operations, 17
  R.A.F. station Berlin, 35, 35M
Germany, Democratic Republic, created, 75
Germany, Federal Republic, created, 75
Gratitude Foundation, creation and charter, 76
Greulich, Gerald G., designs Marston Mat, 43
Ground Control Approach, 32, 47P, 58, 58P
Guilbert, Maj. Edward A., on Tunner's staff, 20

Halvorsen, 1st Lt. Gail S., 62-63, 62P
Hamburg (see Fuhlsbüttel)
Hamman, Lieut. Vernon, Clay Pigeon, 14
Handley Page Halifax/Halton
  Machat, 48, 49; Specifications 48
  Skyflight, 31P
  Eagle Aviation, Lancashire Aircraft Corp., B.A.A.S., Westminster Airways, 48P
  World Air Freight, Bond Air Services, 49P
  Extensive use at Fuhlsbüttel, 38
  Last civilian sortie into Berlin, 48
  Used as oil tanker, and to carry salt, 48, 53P
  B.O.A.C. Conversion, 49
  Fleet record, 49T
  British independent airline fleets, 57T
  Fatal crashes, 67T
Handley Page Hastings
  R.A.F. fleet, 16, 21, 56P
  Operations from Schleswigland, 38
  Fatal crash, 67T
  Aircraft preserved at Gatow, 76
Harper, Flt. Lt. D.J., last mission from Schleswigland, 38
Harris, Capt. Clifford, short notice relocation, 61
Havel Lake (Havelsee), Berlin marine base for flying boats, 31, 39, 54P
Heimlich, William F., director, Berlin radio, 72
Historical Foundation, Berlin Aircraft, 77
Hope, Bob, entertains troops, 64
Hornton Airways, British charter company
  Douglas Dakota, 55P; Fleet list, 57T
Howgozit
  Vittles record keeping, 59, 59P
Howley, Gen. Frank
  Controls 'Milk Run,' 17
  Reviews Airlift achievement, 74
Huebner, Maj. Gen. C. R., controls 'Milk Run,' 17

Internal German Service (I.G.S.), A.O.A., 44
I.R.C. (International Red Cross), relief work, 60

Johnstone, A.M., R.A.F. pilot, first at Tegel, 35
Kearsley Airways, British charter company
  Lone survivor, 56; Fleet list, 57T
Kelly AFB, San Antonio, engine overhauls, 40
Kemper, Capt. George A., commands C-82 fleet, 27
Keys, Clement, perceptive commentary, 41
Knicker, Operation
  Early British Airlift, 16, 18
  Special dispensation, 18
  First supplies from Wunstorf, 37
Korean War, airlift record compared, 75
K.P.D. (German Communist Party), 11
Kurhaus, converted as services amenity, 36

Laker, Freddie, supplies Bond Air Services, 49
Lancashire Aircraft Corp., British charter company
  At Schleswigland, 38
  Halton aircraft, as tanker, 48P, 53P
  Fleet list, 57T
Latter Day Saints (Mormons), relief work, 60
LeMay, Lt. Gen. Curtis E., Commander in Chief U.S.A.F.E.
  Initiates Berlin Airlift, 16, 17P
  Promoted and replaced, 30
Lindsey Air Station, honors Airlift victims, 76
Liquid Fuel Freighters 53T
Little Vittles Operation, 62-63
Lockheed Aircraft Service Corp., maintenance, 40
Lockheed C-5A Galaxy, load capability, 75
Lockheed F-80 Shooting Star, in Germany, 15
Lübeck, R.A.F. Station, 38, 38M
Ludiow, Kathryn, first WAF assigned to Airlift, 69
Ludwig, Prof. Edward, designs Airlift Memorial, 76
Luftwaffe, Stalingrad airlift compared, 75
Lutz, Karl, designs memorial window, 76

McMahon, Lt. Col. Orval O., on Tunner's staff, 20
Maintenance
  Review of Airlift organization, 40-41
  Working conditions, 61P
Marshall Plan, 13
Marston Mat, origin of P.S.P., **43**
Medal for Human Action, awarded, 74
Memorials, Airlift, 76, 76P
Merer, Air Commodore J.W. F., British Deputy to Gen. Tunner, 20P, 30
Middletown, PA, Airlift spare parts supply, 40
Military Airlift Command, lifespan dates, 75
Military Air Transport Service (MATS)
  Created in 1948, 46
  Provides aircraft to U.S.A.F.E., 30
  Summary of Squadrons, 30T
  Lifespan dates, 75
Milton, Col. Theodore, on Tunner's staff, 20
Mobile snack bar, 61P
Molitov-Ribbentrop Pact, 10
Moore, Garry, N.B.C. Show, 64
Moravia, German protectorate, 10
Mormons, relief work, 60
M.S.C. (Menonite Assistance), relief work,60

Naval Air Transport Service (**NATS**)
  Fleet transfer from Pacific Theater, 29M
  Merges with A.T.C., 46
  VR-6, VR-8, U.S. Navy squadrons, 29, 68
Nelson, Orvis, heads Transocean Air Lines, 45
New Yorker, Magazine, summarizes Airlift effort, 78
New Zealand Air Force, Royal, 31, 38
North Atlantic Treaty Organization (NATO), created, 75

Oberpfaffenhofen
  Maintenance base, 39, 39P, 40, 41P
Oder-Neisse Line, 10
OMGUS (Office of Military Government, U.S.), 12
Operation Bird Dog, 13
Orns, Pfc. Johnny, killed by aircraft landing, 66
Over 21, Connie Bennett Show, 64

Pan American Airways, participation in Airlift, 44
Paterson, Operation, early British Airlift, 16
Plainfare, Operation, British Airlift
  Begins, 16, 31
  Summary of freight and passengers carried, 58
Pointer, ADC Sidney, rescue commendation, 66
Poland, German invasion; regains nationhood, 10
'Polish Corridor', 10
Potsdam Agreement, 11
Price, Capt. George, Pan Am pilot, 44
Provide Promise, Yugoslav airlift compared, 75
P.S.P. (Pierced Steel Planking)
  Development of temporary runway surface, **43**, 43P, 79P
  At Gatow, 1946, 35; Tegel, 1948, 35; Celle, 37; Fuhlsbüttel, Lübeck, Schleswigland, 38

Quartered City, movie film, 64

Radio and Radio Range Beacons, (M/F), 32
Rear Airlift Supply Organization (RASO), 17
Red Eagle, **Machat 48**, 48P
Reuter, Ernst
  Lord Mayor of Berlin, 6P; 11
  Mobilizes Berliners, 70
  Celebration speech, 74
Rhein-Main A.B., Frankfurt
  Main Airlift operations base, 19P, **36**, 36M, 36P
  Central maintenance depot, 40
  Memorial, 76; Historical exhibit, 77
R.I.A.S., Berlin radio station, 72
Robertson, Sir Brian, British Military Governor Germany, 17
Royal Air Force
  Starts Operations Knicker, Paterson, 16, 18
  Starts Operation Plainfare, 31, 78
  Builds runway at Gatow, 35
  Wunstorf, Fassberg airfield operations, 37
  Lays P.S.P. runway at Celle, 37; 42P
  At Hamburg, Lübeck, Schleswigland, 38
  Sunderland aircraft, 39; **Machat, 54**
  Distance measuring equipment (D.M.E.), 47
  Forms Civil Airlift Division, 56
  Ends operations, 74, 74T
Royal Army Service Corps (RASC), 17P, 18P
Royal Australian Air Force, 31, 38
Royal New Zealand Air Force, 31, 38
Royal South African Air Force, 31, 38
Russell, Jane, entertains troops, 64
Russia, invasions, 9

Santa Claus, operation from Fassberg, 37
Schleswigland, R.A.F. Station, **38**, 38M
Schroeder, Frau Louise, Mayor of Berlin, 6P
Schuffert, TSgt. Jack, cartoonist, 65
Scott AFB, memorial, 76
Scottish Airlines
  Consolidated B-24 Liberator, 52, **Machat, 53**
  Douglas Dakota, 55P
  Fleet list, 57T
'Scrambled Egg,' 17
Seaboard and Western Airlines
  Participates in Airlift, 45
  Machat C-54, 45
  CARE shipments, 60
S.E.D (Socialist Unity Party), 11
Short Hythe (civilian conversion of Sunderland)
  Development, 54
  Aquila Airways fleet, 57T
Short Sunderland
  Machat, Specification, 54
  R.A.F. fleet, 16
  Anodized hull to carry salt, 31
  Operations from Finkenwerder to Havel Lake, Berlin, 39
Silver City Airways
  Bristol Freighter, **Machat**, 56
  Fleet list, 57T
Sivewright Airways, fleet list, 57T
Skyflight, fleet list, 57T
Skyways
  Operates from Wunstorf, 37
  Lancastrian tankers, 52
  Fleet list, 57T
Slaker, Capt. Kenneth, survives crash, 66
Sleighbells, project, Christmas toys, 60P
Smith, Brig. Gen. Joseph, commands and names Airlift, 16
Sokolowsky, Marshall Vassily, Soviet Military Governor
  Walks out of Allied Control Council, 13
  Initiates blockade, 15; Caught speeding, 16
South African Air Force, Royal
  Supplies squadron, 31, 38
  Berlin Airlift Reunion Committee, 77
Soviet harassment, summary of incidents, 73T
S.P.D.(Social Democratic Party), 11
Spirit of Freedom, The, flying museum 77, 77P
S.R.C. (Swiss Red Cross), relief work, 60
Stars and Stripes, Schuffert cartoons, 65
Statistics
  Dates of U.S. Armed forces arrival, 30T
  British Halifax/Halton fleet and record, 49T
  British civilian Tudor/York fleet and record, 51T
  Liquid fuel aircraft and record, 53T
  British civil Dakota tonnages, 55T
  British charter airlines, complete fleet and record, 57T
  American, British casualties, 66T; 67T
  Airlift cost analysis, 69T
  Location of individual U.S. Air Force units, 69T
  Incidents of Soviet harassment, 73T
  Dates of airfield closures, 74T
  Summary of tonnages, 79T
Steber, Lt. Clarence, survives crash, 66
Sudetenland, annexed by Germany, 10
Swallwell, Col. Kenneth E., on Tunner's staff, 20
Swedish Red Cross, relief work, 60
Symington, Stuart, Secretary of the Air Force visits Airlift bases, 40, 64

Take It or Leave It, N.B.C. Show, 64
Tanker Association, Airlift, memorializes Airlift, 77
Task Force Times 20, 59; Schuffert cartoons, 65
Tegel
  Airfield in French Sector, 35, 35M
  Runway construction, 42P
Tempelhof
  Berlin Airport, **34**, 34M, 34P
  Runway construction, 42P
Texas Eng. and Mfg. Co., overhaul base, 40
Third Reich, 10M
Thompson, 1st Lt. William G., on Tunner's staff, edits *Task Force Times*, 20
Transocean Air Lines Inc.
  Airlift maintenance, 40
  Participates in Airlift, 45
  Machat C-54, 45
Transworld Charter, fleet list, 57T
Travis AFB, Museum, 77
Trent Valley Aviation, fleet list, 57T
Trezona, F.I., pilot of tragic crash, 67
Troop Carrier Command, supplies aircraft, 30T
Truman, Harry S
  Commemorates Army Air Force, 13
  Establishes Marshall Plan, 13
  Orders transfer of Boeing B-29s, 15
Tunner, Lt. Gen. William H.
  Takes command of Airlift, 20, 20P
  Track record in China, 20, 20M
  Flies in C-97, 28
  Comments on Airlift operations, 30
  Emphasized good maintenance, 40
  Observes maintenance at Oberpfaffenhofn, 41P
  'Jungle Drums,' 46
  Over the Hump, book authorship, quotation, 59
  Comments on soldiers life, 61
  Reports on removal of obstruction at Tegel, 73
  Commands airlift in Korean War, 75
  Buried in Arlington National Cemetery, 75
  Bronze bust at Scott AFB, 76
T.W.A. (Transcontinental & Western Air), participates in Airlift, 44

UNICEF, relief work, 60
Union Club, Celle, 37
Union Operation, Christmas party, 58
U.S. Air Force
  Created, 1947, 13
  Locates C-54s at Fassberg and Celle, 37
  Complete list of units in Airlift, 69T
  Statistical summary of Airlift costs, 69T
  Museum at Wright-Patterson AFB, 77
U.S.A.F.E (U.S. Air Forces in Europe)
  Redesignation, 14
  Ends operations, 74
U.S. Army Europe, review of units supporting the Airlift, 68, 68P
U.S. Navy
  Review of Airlift contribution, 29, 68
  Sea Lift, aviation fuel shipped to Bremerhaven, 69
  Celebrates end of Blockade, 78P

Vandenberg, Gen. Hoyt, appoints Gen. Tunner to command Airlift, 20
Veronika-Invasion, 37
Veterans Association, Berlin Airlift, (BAVA), memorializes Airlift, 77
Vickers Viking
  Trans World Charter, 57T, 57P
  Buzzed by Yak-3 and crashes, 73
Vittles, Operation
  U.S. Airlift, 16, 78
  Builds up fleet, 30
  Daily quotas, 59
Vittles Varieties, entertainment for troops, 64
Von Rohden, Maj. Gen. Hans Detlev, solves maintenance problem, 40

Wannsee, branch of Lake Havel, 54P
Warsaw Pact, formation, 75
Weisner, Hugo, saves Fassberg A.B., 37
Weitzenbruch, former name for Celle A.B., 37
Westminster Airways, British charter company
  At Schleswigland, 38
  Halifax aircraft, 48P
  Fleet list, 57T
Wiesbaden, U.S. Air Force base, 36, 36M
Wiessenrieder, H. glassmaster, crafts memorial window, 76
Wiggly Wings, Uncle (Gail Halverson), 63
Williams, Capt. Eugene, T., maintains Operation Little Vittles, 63
Wooten, James, heads Alaska Airlines, 45
'Workhorse Harry,' veteran C-54, 45
World Air Freight, British charter company
  At Fuhlsbüttel, 38
  Halifax aircraft, 49P
  Fleet list, 57T
Wright Field, role in Airlift spare parts supply, 40
Wright-Patterson AFB, USAF Museum, 77
Wunstorf, R.A.F. Airfield, **37**, 37M

Yarde, Grp. Capt.
  Station commander, Gatow, 35
  Solves bird-strike problem, 59
Yakolev Yak-3, hassles Airlift aircraft, 73

Zeppelinheim, village confiscated, 36
Zhukov, Marshall Georgi K., Soviet Commander in Germany, 14

[P=Photograph; M=Map; T=Table]